ROUTLEDGE LIBRARY EDITIONS:
RENAISSANCE DRAMA

Volume 3

ENCHANTED SHOWS

# ENCHANTED SHOWS
Vision and Structure in Elizabethan and Shakespearean Comedy About Magic

ELISSA HARE

LONDON AND NEW YORK

First published in 1988 by Garland Publishing, Inc.

This edition first published in 2017
by Routledge
2 Park Square, Milton Park, Abingdon, Oxon OX14 4RN

and by Routledge
711 Third Avenue, New York, NY 10017

*Routledge is an imprint of the Taylor & Francis Group, an informa business*

© 1988 Elissa Hare

All rights reserved. No part of this book may be reprinted or reproduced or utilised in any form or by any electronic, mechanical, or other means, now known or hereafter invented, including photocopying and recording, or in any information storage or retrieval system, without permission in writing from the publishers.

*Trademark notice*: Product or corporate names may be trademarks or registered trademarks, and are used only for identification and explanation without intent to infringe.

*British Library Cataloguing in Publication Data*
A catalogue record for this book is available from the British Library

ISBN: 978-1-138-71372-7 (Set)
ISBN: 978-1-315-19807-1 (Set) (ebk)
ISBN: 978-1-138-23494-9 (Volume 3) (hbk)
ISBN: 978-1-138-23495-6 (Volume 3) (pbk)
ISBN: 978-1-315-30591-2 (Volume 3) (ebk)

**Publisher's Note**
The publisher has gone to great lengths to ensure the quality of this reprint but points out that some imperfections in the original copies may be apparent.

**Disclaimer**
The publisher has made every effort to trace copyright holders and would welcome correspondence from those they have been unable to trace.

# Enchanted Shows

Vision and Structure
in Elizabethan and Shakespearean
Comedy About Magic

Elissa Hare

GARLAND PUBLISHING, INC.
NEW YORK & LONDON 1988

Copyright © 1988
Elissa Hare
All Rights Reserved

**Library of Congress Cataloging-in-Publication Data**

Hare, Elissa Beatrice.
Enchanted shows.
(Garland publications in American and English literature)
Originally published as the author's thesis (Ph.D.—Princeton, 1985)
Bibliography : p.
1. English drama—Early modern and Elizabethan, 1500-1600—History and criticism. 2. Magic in literature. 3. English drama (Comedy)—History and criticism. 4. Shakespeare, William, 1564-1616—Comedies. I. Title. II. Series.
PR658.M27H37 1988      822'.3'0937      88-16460
ISBN 0-8240-6393-7

Printed on acid-free, 250-year-life paper
Manufactured in the United States of America

... & then this appearance was no more, but I found myself sitting on a pleasant bank beside a river by moonlight, hearing a harper, who sung to the harp ...

Blake, "The Marriage of Heaven and Hell"

Table of Contents

Preface and Acknowledgments                                    v

Chapter I        The fabric of this vision:               1
                 magic illusion, time, and space

Chapter II       "More than magic can perform":          29
                 Greene and Peele

Chapter III      Over-reaching fantasies:                62
                 Marlovian magic

Chapter IV       Anticipating the promised end:          91
                 magical discontinuity in
                 A Midsummer Night's Dream

Chapter V        Shakespeare's dissolving magic:        138
                 The Tempest

Works Cited                                             191

Preface and Acknowledgments

The original inspiration for this study came in a year-long undergraduate seminar on Spenser and Milton with Alexander Leggatt at the University of Toronto. I owe much of my own ideas on the structures of romance in drama to his reading of The Faerie Queene, which I attempt to acknowledge in my title and introductory pages. I am even more in debt to the care and perceptiveness with which my two advisors, Lawrence Danson and Alvin Kernan, read the manuscript, in all its incarnations. Anything I learned about the process of composition is to their credit. Any inadequacies of the end result are my own. I would like also to thank my friends and my family for their encouragement, support, and patience, and lastly, thank new friends for new ideas.

# Chapter I

## The fabric of this vision: magic illusion, time, and space

Moments of clear, incontrovertible vision are few, as each of us privately knows only too well. What is worse is that the most rare visions are notoriously short-lived, their value, perversely, being inversely proportionate to their duration. Had we but world enough and time, the reticence of Calidore's Graces in Book Six of The Faerie Queene, for example,[1] might seem less disappointing, but as things are, Calidore's tantalizingly brief glimpse stands as a sorry reminder of our attempts to see into the truth and to fix it in our mind's eye. The "enchaunted show" (VI.x.17) Calidore confronts disappears the instant it is witnessed, as if the mutual act of seeing destroys the vision:

> soone as he appeared to their vew,
> They vanisht all away out of his sight,
> And cleane were gone, which way he never knew.
> (VI.x.18)

Fairy knight and shepherd piper are left lamenting, and Colin Clout chides the intruder for chasing the scene's graces away. So might poet chastize his more naive

---

[1] All quotations are to Edmund Spenser, The Faerie Queene, ed. T.P. Roche, Jr., (New Haven: Yale Univ. Press, 1978).

observers for their voyeuristic penetration of his creative inspiration.[2]

Recalling Colin's rebuke might seem an inauspicious beginning to a study of enchanted shows by Shakespeare, Greene, and Peele. But Calidore's experience crystallizes for me the central intuition of romantic comedy, where the dramatists, too, discover graces in nature, graces that, though fragile and elusive, ultimately amend that nature. Romantic comedy at once imitates and improves upon the "realities" of our natural world; it works miraculous changes in the lives of its characters, and its happy ending suggests the advent of a transformed, and most desirable, state of being.

An art that thus envisions a better nature, substitutes gold for dross, requires a certain kind of dramatic structure: in a dramatic world where miracles are the order of the day, progress is naturally unpredictable. Transitions in romantic comedy between one setting or situation to another are abrupt and surprising; the movement of characters through time and space is inadequately prepared and cursorily justified by any realistic standard. Shakespeare and the University Wits debate the extent to which the deliberate violation

---

[2] A. Bartlett Giamatti, "Spenser: From Magic to Miracle," in Four Essays in Romance, ed. Herschel Baker (Cambridge: Harvard Univ. Press, 1971), describes Spenser's own linguistic efforts to fix moments of revelation.

of realistic expectation in their comedies can cumulatively give intimations of the ideal. This chapter introduces the way in which Friar Bacon and Friar Bungay, The Old Wives Tale, the generically anomalous Doctor Faustus, A Midsummer Night's Dream, and The Tempest,[3] all rationalize the unrealism and improbabilities typical of romantic comedy as miracles wrought by specifically magic intervention. The stage-magicians of these plays, acting with more or less consistency and competence as authorial surrogates, bear considerable responsibility for the prevailing discontinuities of dramatic action. The magician, like his author, subjects the developing action to bizarre twists and turns, commanding characters, places, and scenes instantaneously to materialize and abruptly to disappear. The shows put on by the magician often confuse beyond repair his audience's ability to distinguish truth from illusion. Magic, in short, works like the dramatist's imagination, to amend nature. This handful of plays

[3] All Shakespeare quotations are from The Arden Shakespeare, gen. eds., Harold F. Brooks, Harold Jenkins, and Brian Morris; they are specified as they appear; thus Shakespeare, A Midsummer Night's Dream, ed. Harold F. Brooks (London: Methuen, 1979); The Tempest, ed. Frank Kermode (London: Methuen, 1954, 58); Robert Greene, Friar Bacon and Friar Bungay, ed. Daniel Seltzer (Lincoln: Univ. of Nebraska Press, 1963) is the edition of that play from which I quote; George Peele, The Old Wives Tale, ed. Frank S. Hook, in The Dramatic Works of George Peele, vol. 3 of The Life and Works of George Peele, general ed. Charles T. Prouty (New Haven: Yale Univ. Press, 1970); my citations of Doctor Faustus are to the conjectural reconstruction of the B-text by W. W. Greg, ed., Marlowe's Doctor Faustus, 1604-1616: Parallel Text (Oxford: Clarendon Press, 1950).

explicitly about magic, and identified by George Hibbard as "magical comedy...a distinct sub-species" of Shakespearean comedy,[4] allows the dramatists a unique opportunity to express their habitual comic orientation towards poesis rather than mimesis. Contemporary discussion of the principles behind sympathetic magic and artistic imagination reveal, as this introductory chapter will explain, striking similarities: each is the attempt to realize a desire, to construct what is lacking in the natural world. There is, however, no satisfactory critical elucidation of the connection between the magician's influence on <u>structure</u> in romantic comedy and the artist's constructive <u>vision</u>.[5] Nor is there, either, much help in

[4] G. R. Hibbard, "Adumbrations of <u>The Tempest</u> in <u>A Midsummer Night's Dream</u>," <u>Shakespeare Survey</u>, 31 (1978), 78.

[5] Alvin Kernan, <u>The Playwright as Magician</u> (New Haven: Yale Univ. Press, 1979), provides the best analysis of the context of dramatic magic in Elizabethan and Jacobean intellectual and social history; for the best of the source-hunters see Robert Rentoul Reed, Jr., <u>The Occult on the Tudor and Stuart Stage</u> (Boston: Christopher Publishing House, 1965), designed as a corrective to studies that show what the drama tells about magic instead of the reverse; see, e.g., Robert Hunter West, <u>The Invisible World: A Study of Pneumatology in Elizabethan Drama</u> (Athens, GA: Univ. of Georgia Press, 1939), and his <u>Shakespeare and the Outer Mystery</u> (Lexington: Univ. of Kentucky Press, 1968); K. M. Briggs, <u>Pale Hecate's Team</u> (London: Routledge and Kegan Paul, 1962); David Woodman, <u>White Magic and Elizabethan Renaissance Drama</u> (Rutherford: Fairleigh Dickinson Univ. Press, 1973), discusses broad thematic significances of magic in a handful of plays; two miscellaneous studies worth mentioning are Paul Arnold, <u>Esoterisme de Shakespeare</u> (Paris: Mercure de France, 1955), and his <u>Clef Pour Shakespeare: Esoterisme de L'oeuvre Shakespearienne</u> (Paris: Librarie Philosophique J. Vrin, 1977).

the criticism on the renunciation of magic that
unfailingly concludes the dramatic enterprise.
Contemporary ambivalence about the morality of magic
seems to have imposed on our playwrights the obligation
to undermine the principle on which their own vision and
structure was largely based. This dissertation examines
the degree of identification between artist and magician in
the plays already mentioned by Greene, Peele, Marlowe, and
Shakespeare. This means investigating both the extent to
which dramatic structure is conditioned by magic, and the
extent to which the dramatist's vision is compromised as he
is forced by external pressures to modify his synthesis of
magic with poetic art. The remainder of this chapter,
after illustrating some representative structural
discontinuities in the plays, sketches the literary
controversy abut miracles and verisimilitude in art, and
the more general controversy about magic in sixteenth-
century Europe, in order to provide preliminary explanation
of both the use and the renunciation of magic in English
stage plays.

The most obvious illustration of deliberate departures
from mimetic representation is the persistent illogic of
dramatic progress in the plays. A few examples may show
that sequence does not obey the law of cause and effect,
and that in most cases magic "explains" the disturbance
of temporal flow and dislocations of place. Faustus'

extensive journeys through various epochs and empires, which do at least as much as textual irregularity to align the play with what Bernard Beckerman calls the "extensive" mode of dramatic construction,[6] are enabled by the art of magic. Friar Bacon's magic interrupts a wedding, halts the thrust of swords, and transfers characters like the Hostess of the Bell at Henley bodily into his Oxford study. When we turn to The Old Wives Tale we again find close connection between magic and temporal structure: the method of Sacrapant's interference with time so closely resembles those temporal disturbances not accomplished by the magician, that magic seems implicit throughout. Compare for example Sacrapant's resurrection of Huanebango with Peele's resurrection of Jack. Space, too, appears magically fluid, as distance and physical perspective undergo bizarre permutations: when characters dig to a light under a hill, and when a mysterious head emerges from the bottom of a well, it becomes clear that landscape, and indeed all physical matter and forms, are as malleable as time itself is in these plays. Nowhere, in fact, does magic make its presence felt as forcefully as when suddenly ridding the stage of the material objects and presences

---

[6] Bernard Beckerman, Dynamics of Drama: Theory and Method of Analysis (1970; rpt. New York: Drama Book Specialist, 1979) pp. 188-89, identifies Shakespearean dramatic structure as extensive, since its time and space are not subject to the compression of the Aristotelian formula, and its "action is journey rather than confrontation."

that magic itself has conjured into view. The magicians of romantic comedy, like the dramatists themselves, play endless variations on the theme of the disappearing moment, the continually vanishing scene; it is thus that they pursue their obsession with illusion. Friar Bacon, Prospero, and even Oberon, are not content merely to put on magic shows. They must also demonstrate the power of their magic by revealing the illusoriness of their shows, usually by causing the illusions to vanish as spectacularly as they have materialized. Bacon, in Greene's relatively crude dramatic venture, merely <u>tells</u> us that the Suffolk scenes visible in his glass are illusions, when he prevents Edward from stabbing Lacy in the glass. Or he exhibits the fragility of others' illusions by making Bungay's apparitions (and Bungay) vanish into thin air. Faustus, a more sophisticated exemplar of the art, trades on the tendency of illusions to dissolve, and sells the horse-courser an animal that disintegrates in water.

Shakespeare recognizes in similar fashion the inherent instability in dramatic illusions of real time, space, and material presence. <u>The Tempest</u> proceeds by the sudden materializing and dissolving of magic illusions: the dissolving directly serves the magician's didactic purpose. These continually interrupt the temporal and spatial continuity which, notes Susanne Langer, is the chief illusion of more mimetic art.[7] There is, for example, the disappearing banquet of III.iii, brought in by Prospero's spirits, "strange shapes" (s.d. 18) that "strangely" vanish (III.iii.39). It is the abrupt whisking away of the feast under the very eyes of Alonso and his court, more than its initial presentation for them, that constitutes the moral warning and that contributes to their eventual redemption. But not all the habitual interruption of illusion in The Tempest adequately prepares us for the moment in Act IV when the marriage masquers "heavily vanish" with a "strange, hollow, and confused noise" (s.d. IV.i.138). The masquers have celebrated the fruits of the ground, "Earth's increase, foison plenty" (110), and all that sustains bodily life. But these actors, paradoxically, are all spirits, and

> Are melted into air, into thin air:
> And, like the baseless fabric of this vision,
> The cloud-capp'd towers, the gorgeous palaces,
> The solemn temples, the great globe itself,
> Yea, all which it inherit, shall dissolve,
> And, like this insubstantial pageant faded,
> Leave not a rack behind.  (IV.i.150-56)

The process is literally disincarnation, flesh become words.

Again and again the enchanted shows of and within Shakespearean comedy disintegrate into nothingness, and the ruptures of time and space disprove our perceptions of

---

[7] Susanne Langer, Feeling and Form: A Theory of Art (New York: Scribner's, 1953), pp. 77, 88-39, 110.

9

substance and material truths, proving all to be illusions, and essentially impermanent. Theseus may perhaps be forgiven his limited appreciation of poetic enterprise as the imaginative bodying forth of "the forms of things unknown" (V.i.15); the poet, like the magician, habitually "turns" the things he desires, but does not yet possess, to shapes, and "gives to airy nothing/A local habitation and a name" (16-17). Shakespeare's poetic genius, and his magic, consists in seeing more than this conventional wisdom. The center of A Midsummer Night's Dream, and the whole of The Tempest, dramatize nothing else if not the instability of magic illusions. The four lovers of the forest outside Athens collectively constitute an identity that is highly fluid; individually they demonstrate no fixed shape at all. The play is a prolonged fantasia not so much on the shape-changing of classical metamorphosis (though that is involved) as on shape-blurring (concentrating on the instant of transformation). The physical lineaments of Demetrius' and Lysander's forms are not only interchangeable, but actually exchanged, as, moment by moment, different identities occupy the same body.

What we have then is the willed and repeated collapse of physical definition, and thus of a basic dramatic law: you must have the body.[8] Getting bodies of such frailty from

[8] Michael Goldman, Shakespeare and the Energies of Drama (Princeton: Princeton Univ. Press, 1972), p. 4, describes the "unique focus on the body" as "the crucially distinctive character of dramatic experience."

10

one point to the next in the course of dramatic action is a hazardous enterprise, especially given the bewildering, fluid benavior of dramatic space and time. The concrete and the disembodied states, the real and the illusory, are disconcertingly interchangeable, as actions and visions, scenes, and shows within shows vanish as fast as they appear: each novelty cancels the last. The laws of physics become merely superficial counters in a dramatic game of chance and daring. These are "th'ill customes of the age" on which Ben Jonson poured scorn. His 1616 Prologue to Every Man in His Humour is an attack on the impulse of Shakespearean comedy[9]

> To make a child, now swadled, to proceede
> Man, and then shoote up, in one beard, and weede,
> Past three score yeeres: or, with three rustie
> swords,
> And Helpe of some few foot-and-half-foote words,
> Fight over Yorke, and Lancasters long iarres:
> And in the tyring-house bring wounds, to scarres.
> He rather prayes, you will be pleas'd to see
> One such, to day, as other playes should be.
> Where neither Chorus wafts you ore the seas;
> Nor creaking throne comes down, the boyes to
> please,'
> Nor nimble squibbe is seene, to make afear'd
> The gentlewomen; nor roul'd bullet heard
> To say, it thunders, nor tempestuous drumme
> Runbles, to tell you when the storme doth come;
> But deeds and language, such as men doe use:
> And persons, such as Comoedie would chuse,
> When she would shew an Image of the times,
> And sport with humane follies, not with crimes.
> (7-24)

[9] Ben Jonson, Every Man in His Humour, [1616], in Ben Jonson, eds. C. H. Herford, Percy Simpson, and Evelyn Simpson, vol. 3 (Oxford: Clarendon Press, 1927).

When the Elizabethan comic playwright deliberately submitted time and space to the tricks of strong imagination, he was playing to an audience that knew the options.

Jonson's preference for drama that "would shew an Image of the times" is illustrated in his more mimetic magic comedy, The Alchemist, which contains none of the temporal and spatial surprises typical of the Shakespearean alternative.[10] Rather it is a satire on gulls who believe the improbable efficacy of "magicians." Face and Subtle plot much of the play's action for their author, Jonson, but the analogue between "magician" and artist is wholly unlike the Shakespearean model. Shakespeare's magicians are either frivolous or serious exploiters of happenstance; Jonson's "magicians" are cheap tricksters whose magic is a pretense and whose control of the intrigues, at once more cynical and total than that of Shakespeare's magicians, inevitably leads to their own subordination in the conclusion. Shakespeare's final subjection of the magician is by contrast an evitable result of the magician's frailty, something that is imposed on the ending rather than a logical outgrowth of the play's progress. Shakespeare's magic is "real" and has an independent life. My use of the term "magical comedy" should be understood as excluding Jonson's drama.

[10] Ben Jonson, The Alchemist, in Ben Jonson, ed. C.H. Herford and Percy Simpson, vol. 5 (Oxford: Clarendon Press, 1937).

12

The fundamental disagreement between Jonson and Shakespeare about the use of magic, miracle, and unrealistic treatment of nature, time and space, is reflected in the central literary controversy of the period. Both in Italy and in England critics debated the extent to which marvels, enchantments, and improbabilities were permissible in art.[11] In Italy the argument centered around Ariosto and Tasso; in England Sidney took up the cudgels against such excesses as Jonson condemns in Shakespeare. It is worth taking a look at the main Italian positions before going on to the situation in England, as the Italian material is a useful introduction; it is, indeed, dangerous to assume that the Italian controversy, at its height during the last two decades of the sixteenth century, went completely unnoticed by the English dramatists. Greene dramatized _Orlando Furioso_, and whether or not he worked independently of Harington's 1591 translation, he must have had an idea of contemporary estimates of Ariosto's plot: at the very least he could have got it from Harington's notes.[12] Shakespeare probably read Cinthio's _Gli Hecatommithi_ (containing the

[11] For an excellent concise discussion of contemporary balances of mimesis and poesis see Baxter Hathaway, _Marvels and Commonplaces: Renaissance Literary Criticism_ (New York: Random House, 1968), esp. pp 43-132.

[12] Robert Greene, _Orlando Furioso_, in _The Plays and Poems of Robert Greene_, ed. J. Churton Collins, vol. 1 (Oxford: Clarendon Press, 1905); Robert McNulty, ed., Ariosto, _Orlando Furioso_, tr. into English heroical verse by Sir John Harington [1591] (Oxford: Clarendon Press, 1972), p.xxvi, advises that "to doubt at least a reading knowledge of the language in any educated Elizabethan is dangerous."

source of Othello) in the Italian,[13] and Cinthio was a key contributor to the pro-Ariosto camp. There can be little doubt that the substance of the Tasso-Ariosto conflict was in the air on Bankside, even if the dramatic as opposed to epic treatment of marvels and magic owed little to direct Italian influence.[14]

The Italians were unified in connecting the distortion of time and space in romance plots with the marvelous and magical operations described in those plots. Even Tasso and his supporters, holding more closely to the Aristotelian rules, could commend plays "full of variety and inconstancy, inundated with strange and unexpected accidents -- from which come the marvelous."[15] But critics were polarized between the limited marvels and improbabilities of Gerusalemme Liberata and what many saw as their excessive use in Ariosto.[16]

[13] Alvin Kernan, ed., Othello, in The Complete Signet Classic Shakespeare, gen. ed. Sylvan Barnet (New York: Harcourt, 1972), p. 1094, and Frank Kermode, ed., Othello, in The Riverside Shakespeare, gen. ed. G. Blakemore Evans (Boston: Houghton Mifflin, 1974), p. 1198, agree that in the absence of a contemporary English translation, Shakespeare more probably used the original Italian version of Cinthio than the 1584 translation of Gabriel Chappuys.

[14] For a full discussion of the central and ubiquitous importance of the controversy to sixteenth-century literary thinking see Bernard Weinberg, A History of Literary Criticism in the Italian Renaissance (Chicago: Univ. of Chigago Press, 1961), vol. 2, pp. 954-1073.

[15] Paolo Beni, Comparazione di Omero, Virgilio e Torquato, in Tasso, Opere (Pisa, 1828), XXII, 238-39, cited in Hathaway, Marvels and Commonplaces, pp. 130-31.

[16] See e.g. Weinberg, A History, p.955:"The

14

Cinthio, less rigidly bound by Aristotelian mimetic

standards, defends impossible things such as "The changing

of men into trees, of ships into nymphs, of boughs into

ships" because "Such is the quality of the fictional that

often the fables and the untruths though false and

impossible, have more verisimiltude than the factual and the

possible."[17] But it is Sidney, in England, who carves out

with most firmness the middle ground between the two Italian

camps. He refuses to countenance such oddities as Cinthio

describes, and yet defends poetry against the charge that it

is "the mother of lies."[18] Sidney's compromise brings him

closer to Shakespeare than the Italians are, and it is

reasonable to suppose that Sidney's ideas lie

Aristotelian objections brought against Ariosto bear upon
two matters, his construction of the plot and his handling
of verisimilitude" ... this included, pp. 956-57, Ariosto's
use of "improbable, marvelous, and supernatural elements."
Beni sanctioned the use of such "supernatural aids" in the
disentangling of plots as "angelic performance or a
miraculous and divine cause" because "these things in kind
are neither impossible nor incredible," but he strongly
deprecated the facile introduction of fairies and magicians,
since these were "entirely feigned or unheard of, or some
virtue is attributed to them as if it were natural, that is
contrary to the course of nature," cited in Hathaway,
Marvels and Commonplaces, p. 130. The last sentence
summarizes the Tasso position: secular magic makes false
claims to naturalness, and only the genuinely natural or
sacred supernatural are admissible in art.

[17] Giraldi Cinthio, Discorso intorno al comporre dei
romanzi, trans. H.L. Snuggs (Lexington: Univ. of Kentucky
Press, 1968), pp. 50-51.

[18] Philip Sidney, The Defence of Poesy, in Sir Philip
Sidney: Selected Prose and Poetry, ed. Robert Kimbrough (San
Francisco: Rinehart, 1969), p. 135; all succeeding
references are to this edition.

behind Shakespearean comedy. A Midsummer Night's Dream and The Tempest reveal not just witty counterattacks against Sidney's demand for unity of time, place, and action, but also a strong bias in favor of Sidney's neoplatonic definition of artistic purpose.

Sidney's defence of fiction as an imitation of divine artistry, creating a second nature and golden world,[19] inadvertently defends romantic comedy also, and particularly the comedies of magic, whose intuition of graces in nature enables nature's amelioration. The dramatists of magical comedy aim to imitate the worker of miracles, locating and drawing out the latent virtues in nature that can make the natural world golden.[20] The close similarity between the work of the sympathetic magician and that of the imaginative artist or dramatist is clearest in Marlowe and Shakespeare; Greene's and Peele's more hesitant identification of art and

[19] Sidney, The Defence of Poesy, p. 108: "Only the poet, disdaining to be tied to any such subjection, lifted up with the vigor of his own invention, doth grow in effect into another Nature, in making things either better than Nature bringeth forth, or, quite anew, forms such as never were in Nature ... Nature never set forth the earth in so rich tapestry as divers poets have done, neither with so pleasant rivers, fruitful trees, sweet- smelling flowers, nor whatsoever else may make the toomuch loved earth more lovely. Her world is brazen, the poets only deliver a golden."

[20] For an expression of this view of Shakespearean comedy see Nevill Coghill, "The Basis of Shakespearian Comedy," in Shakespeare Criticism 1935-60, ed. Anne Ridler (London: Oxford Univ. Press, 1963), pp. 201-27, especially p.210: "Shakespeare began to imagine and explore what we have come to call his 'golden world', taking a phrase of his own from As You Like It."

16

magic precludes the full synthesis of neoplatonic hermetic and aesthetic theory at which Marlowe hints and towards which Shakespeare moves. It is not until The Tempest that the magician is fully licensed to work the plans of his author, and that the contemporary intellectual roots of the analogy between art and magic are finally exposed. The Tempest provides, in its implicit but comprehensive synthesis of Agrippa's defense of sympathetic magic[21] with Sidney's of poetry, a key to the magical comedies (and Marlowe's play) that anticipate it. A brief examination of the connections between Agrippa's and Sidney's thought is thus an indispensable introduction to all the plays.

Magic and imagination typically thrust us outside our experience into the unknown:[22] the poet, aiming like the alchemist to transmute base metal into gold, "making things better than Nature bringeth forth,"[23] follows exactly the same procedures as the practitioner of sympathetic magic, who constructs what he wants to have, in a bid to bring an idea or ideal closer to actuality. "Like produces like," as Frazer notes: if you want your river to teem with fish your

[21] Henry Cornelius Agrippa, The Philosophy of Natural Magic (1531; rpt. Secaucus: University Books, 1974), the first of the three volume De Occulta Philosophia [1533].

[22] Andrew V. Ettin, "Magic into Art: The Magician's Renunciation of Magic in English Renaissance Drama," TSLL, 19 (1977), 273, sees the magician in moral terms as one reaching beyond his individual limitations.

[23] Sidney, The Defence, p. 108; succeeding references are in my text unless otherwise noted.

17

best course is to construct an image of a fish and put it into the water.[24] Theseus, in A Midsummer Night's Dream, unwittingly defines the essence of such magic in his play:

> Such tricks hath strong imagination,
> That if it would  but apprehend some joy,
> It comprehends some bringer of that joy.
> (V.i.18-20)

The fairy magicians, like their author, attempt to forge universal reconciliation and harmony by physically and psychologically rearranging the lovers into the dispositions that will most please all.  Magic, like imagination, comprehends the bringer of the joy it would apprehend.

Karol Berger elaborates the initial spur of this process as the essential lack at the heart of magic and imagination. Speaking of "the importance of the imagination in the magus' world," he writes:  "The essential feature of the imagination is its negativity:  the object that is imagined is not really out there in the external world."[25] As Sidney puts it, with deceptive simplicity:  "Nature never set forth the earth in so rich a tapestry as divers poets have done" (p. 108).

---

[24] J.G. Frazer, The Golden Bough: A Study in Magic and Religion, one-volume abridged edition (New York: Macmillan, 1951), pp. 12, 19-20.

[25] Karol Berger, "Prospero's Art," Shakespeare Studies, 10 (1977), 220-21, speaking here specifically of Prospero but linking Prospero throughout with Renaissance concepts of the magician.

18

But the act of imagining also begins with what is in the real world, as Sidney notes: "There is no art delivered unto mankind that hath not the works of Nature for his principle object, without which they could not consist, and on which they so depend, as they become actors and players, as it were, of what Nature will have set forth" (p. 107). Sidney skilfully disclaims the moral dilemma some find in the conflicting impulses of art towards mimesis and poesis, representation and creation: the poet, he asserts, never lies, because he "never maketh any circles about your imagination, to conjure you to believe for true, what he writeth" (p. 136). Sidney's rigid distinction between art and magic is curious in light of the fact that he was the pupil of one of Agrippa's greatest English followers, Dr. John Dee.[26] Yet Sidney's own description of poetic practice does not so easily separate artist and magician: each ultimately seeks the point of conjunction between his raw material and an idea, between what he has and what he can never quite possess. Art and magic both build on the simultaneous recognition of their difference from and similarity to natural objects and forces.

For if poetry is, as Sidney admits, the art of counterfeiting, of imitation, so is the figuring forth of

---

[26] Frances A. Yates, _Shakespeare's Last Plays: A New Approach_ (London: Routledge, 1975), p. 93.

19

sympathetic magic.[27] As we learn in Agrippa's The Philosophy of Natural Magic (that Agrippa was the conduit by which Shakespeare received Ficinian magical theory, is now a matter of scholarly record),[28] the magician's art is mimetic in two ways. Firstly, the magician constructs an imitation of the desired result in order to achieve it, because he knows that "every thing moves and turns itself to its like" (p. 74). Secondly, the magician's art imitates nature by exploiting sympathies and occult qualities in nature. These are hidden "imbred virtues created by Nature, which we admire and are amazed at, being such as we know not, and indeed seldom or never have seen" (p. 63). The magician inverts the tendency of occult causes to produce "manifest things," by using "things manifest to draw forth things that are occult" (p. 126). He taps the great natural forces of attraction and "mutual correspondency of things among themselves" (p. 124).

[27] Robert Egan, Drama Within Drama (New York: Columbia Univ. Press, 1975), pp. 93-95, also finds the link between magic and art in the "control of reality through imitation"; Northrop Frye frequently notes the mimetic quality of sympathetic magic and its poetic nature, constructing what is desired, see e.g. The Secular Scripture: A Study of the Structure of Romance (Cambridge, Mass.: Harvard Univ. Press, 1976), pp. 35-61.

[28] Succeeding references to The Philosophy of Natural Magic are in my text unless otherwise noted; on the connection between Agrippa's and Shakespeare's thought see Kermode, Arden ed., The Tempest, pp. 142-45; Frances A. Yates, Shakespeare's Last Plays: pp. 93-95; Karol Berger, "Prospero's Art," p. 212; David Woodman, White Magic and English Renaissance Drama pp. 76-77.

20

> If...we would obtain any property or virtue,
> let us seek such animals, or such other things
> whatsoever, in which such a property is in a more
> eminent manner than any other thing, and in these
> let us take that part in which such a property or
> virtue is most vigorous; as if at any time we
> would promote love, let us seek some animal which
> is most loving....(p. 75)

Magic imitates the hidden power of nature to improve itself; it is, as Agrippa notes, fully consonant with neoplatonic theory.[29]

Thus Elizabethans understood that both art and magic could be conceived as simultaneously mimetic and poetic. Magical comedy, like other Renaissance drama, imitates the actions of "real life," but distinguishes itself by allowing persistent departures from realistic presentation, unrealisms out of which may emerge the ideals of the ending. And it is the introduction of temporal, spatial, and physical discontinuities in the dramatic representation of nature that specifically enable the playwright to fuse "real nature" with ideal art.

---

[29] See Agrippa, pp. 65-71, on the connection between the magician's "occult qualities" in matter and neoplatonic ideas; the Florentine Ficinians were also the prime theorists of magic and theurgy of the day. See also Neil H. Wright, "Reality and Illusion as Philosophical Pattern in The Tempest," Shakespeare Studies, 10 (1977), 241-70, for more on the link between poetic and magic theory, and on Prospero as both theurgist and poet creating a "second world" on the island; for a thorough account see D. G. James, The Dream of Prospero (Oxford: Clarendon Press, 1967), pp. 45-71, who sees The Tempest as a farewell to such belief systems.

21

But magic is always renounced or defeated in the dramatic conclusions of romantic comedy. Given the identification between dramatist and magician until those dramatic endings, this raises two questions. Why, first of all, is magic, a clear metonymy for the dramatist's own art, excluded in the end? And secondly, what are the artistic results of such exclusion? I shall deal first with cause, and then with effect. The universal tendency among these dramatists is ultimately to impose modern and familiar conclusions on actions whose development is supernatural and causeless: Greene, Peele, Marlowe, and Shakespeare are all in some way inhibited by the controversy surrounding magic in the sixteenth and seventeenth centuries.

Literary arguments about what was believable and improbable in art reflect debates in the larger contemporary scene. My focus on dramatic vision and structure allows only a glimpse at changes within the larger world picture between 1500 and 1700, but some sketch of these may throw additional light on the drama. Magicians of the early sixteenth century were not easily distinguished from scientists; by 1700, magic and science were poles apart,[30] and even popular as opposed to

[30] C. S. Lewis, English Literature in the Sixteenth Century (London: Oxford Univ. Press, 1954), pp. 5-14, notes the relative lack of differentiation in the sixteenth century between magic in the sixteenth century and the thought of Francis Bacon (a professed enemy of magic): "His endeavor is no doubt contrasted in our minds with that of the magicians: but contrasted only...because we know that

22

merely intellectual allegiances, were slowly shifting from
older to newer methods of compensating for nature's
deficiencies. But even during the period of popular belief
in magic, it was under attack from the Church.

Magicians and clerics were, perhaps understandably, local
rivals for a public urgently beset by problems for which no
modern scientific solutions yet existed; both magic and
religion acknowledged what Robert H. West calls "certain
supra-sensible living essences, which, in the order of God's
providence, sometimes wielded the materials of the physical
world though distinct and separate from them all."[31]
Ecclesiastics warred with particular diligence against their
competition in magicians, and against widespread popular
belief in and even practice of witchcraft, sorcery,
divination, charms, and magic healing. This kind of popular
magic, not to mention learned expositions of and experiments

science succeeded and magic failed. That event was then
still uncertain. Stripping off our knowledge of it, we see
at once that Bacon and the magicians have the closest
possible affinity. Both seek knowledge for the sake of power
... both move in a grandiose dream of days when Man shall
have been raised to the performance of 'all things
possible'"(pp. 13-14; the final quotation is from New
Atlantis). Keith Thomas, Religion and the Decline of Magic
(Harmondsworth: Penguin, 1971, 1973), p. 264, notes that
until the late seventeenth century "the possibility of
certain types of magic was a fundamental presupposition for
most scientists"; he traces, pp. 770-94, the later
separation of magic and science with the advent of the work
of Robert Boyle, William Harvey, and Isaac Newton, though he
believes the decline of magic, oddly, actually preceded the
practical advances if not the theoretical discoveries of
science.

[31] Robert H. West, The Invisible World, p.2.

in the art, were still part of English life a century after the Reformation. Though Protestantism was partly a move to expel superstition from religion, the reformers could not expunge it from the culture: Protestants may, according to Thomas, have made secular magicians _more_ popular and sought after by people whose demand for rituals of a practical efficacy was no longer being met by the Church.[32]

But competition from religion and science still does not fully explain the debilitation of magic in each of its stage appearances. Our dramatists, like sixteenth and seventeenth century magicians, scientists, and exponents of religion, labored in the hope that things could be changed for the better. But such aspiration, equally, carries an implicit recognition of nature's ills. Such a paradox is discernible in our dramatists' treatment of time. The magic, or the imaginative amendment of nature, in romantic comedy is achieved, as we have seen, through its discontinuous temporal progress: but the temporal discontinuity that in magical comedy contributes to happy endings was _in itself_ a subject of acute anxiety in the Renaissance.

---

[32] For a more extensive discussion, see K. Thomas, _Religion and the Decline of Magic_, especially pp. 48, 58, 85-86, 305-18, 326.

Georges Poulet, in <u>Studies</u> <u>in</u> <u>Human</u> <u>Time</u>, describes Renaissance fears about "the discontinuity of duration."[33] Time, in the Reformers' opinion, was incurably double. It offered the hope of redemption in "the continuing act by which a divine unalterable will is superimposed upon a human duration incessantly fading." But at the same time the redeemer subjected man to the threat of extinction:

> the fallen being felt that he lived only from instant to instant and by a miracle. Each instant accorded him was inevitably an instant of collapse. God seemed less to prolong human existence continually than to hold over man from moment to moment an act of vengeance and annihilation.[34]

The temporal discontinuities wrought by magicians on the dramatic action of romantic comedy might similarly be viewed not just as the means of grace and comic resolutions, but also as symptoms of the uneasy human condition. Magicians' control of time and space constantly threatens the continuing existence of their subjects. Temporal discontinuity in magical comedy thus both imitates and deviates from contemporary perceptions of time in the real world. The ambivalence with which Marlowe and Shakespeare, more sophisticated than Greene and Peele, presented magic may owe something to the complex blend of optimism and

[33] Georges Poulet, <u>Studies</u> <u>in</u> <u>Human</u> <u>Time</u>, tr. Elliott Coleman (1956; rpt. NewYork, 1959), p.14.

[34] Poulet, <u>Studies</u> <u>in</u> <u>Human</u> <u>Time</u>, pp. 11-12.

25

pessimism with which Renaissance man regarded the discontinuities of human time itself (though the balance is markedly different in each case).

If such conflicting interpretations of time lie behind the drama, they may well have imposed themselves on it, and the discontinuities of magic time on stage may have aroused discomfort as much on general as on the more literary grounds evinced by contemporary theoreticians of art. That general discomfort has serious consequences for internal dramatic stability. If the magic disruption of time mirrors as much as it distorts Renaissance perceptions of "real" duration, and if the magician like God can withhold as well as guarantee the next moment of human life, then perhaps the curative purpose of the art is jeopardized. It may seem wilful obtuseness to talk of stability in magical comedy, the genre that above all others capitalizes on the instability of our expectations; but the renunciation of magic is properly speaking the rejection of precisely that principle of adventitiousness. Is the final picture of the magician in _Friar_ _Bacon_, _The_ _Old_ _Wives_ _Tale_, _Doctor_ _Faustus_, "the image of the denigrated artist punished for his presumptuousness ... the counterpart of the heroized artist"?[35] The answer seems to me, even in _Doctor_ _Faustus_, to be a resounding no. The problem posed for our dramatists

[35] Ernst Kris and Otto Kurz, _Legend_, _Myth_, _and_ _Magic_ _in_ _the_ _Image_ _of_ _the_ _Artist_, with preface by E.H. Gombrich (New Haven: Yale Univ. Press, 1979), pp. 86-87.

26

lies not in some perceived imperative to apologize for the art, nor even in the need to give new dimensions to what was a standard device in stories of legendary magicians:[36] the dramatists' final abandonment of overt magic in an implicitly magic kind of comedy is in part their attempt to separate salutary from dangerous violations of reality, time, and space, and thus to control potential internal instability by turning it into an explicit conflict.

Greene, Peele, Marlowe, and Shakespeare rationalize their dramatic conclusions, and control their unruly art, with considerable variety of technique and success. Chapter Two examines the indecisive identification by Greene and Peele with, respectively, Friar Bacon and Sacrapant: in these early examples of the genre the magicians' power over time and space, though much like the author's in each case, plays no part in achieving the final improvement on the initial dramatic situation. Chapter Three investigates Marlowe's tragic conception of the magician: Faustus is much closer in spirit to Marlowe, but both are tortured by the paradoxical union of vision and limitation in both magic and imagination. Marlowe's firmer identification of artist-dramatist and magician, I argue, actually reinforces the contradictions of the play. Shakespeare's A Midsummer Night's Dream, the subject of Chapter Four, presents the

---

[36] That is, the renunciation of magic; see D. Woodman, White Magic and English Renaissance Drama, p. 36, for more on this and other standard features, such as the contest between rival magicians.

27

master's version of Greene's and Peele's erratic identification with the magician: here the demonstration of fairy competence is hilariously undercut, and their diminution delicately anticipates Shakespeare's comic intuition that the enchanters' power is greatest when lost.

That innuendo is developed in The Tempest, which provides the Shakespearean answer to the Faustian predicament: Prospero's abjuration of magic redeems him from Faustus' fate. Shakespeare's close identification with Prospero is sufficiently qualified to rescue the play from the subjectivity and emotion that confine Marlowe to tragic antitheses: The Tempest heals the human vulnerabilities exposed by Prospero's art. In Chapter Five I suggest that Shakespeare's crowning achievement in The Tempest is to find, in the very limitations of art and magic, the power that releases imagination: he locates the zenith of magic power at the precise point where magic dissolves. This rationalizes the evanescence of enchanted shows, triumphantly conquering the dilemma that we have so often shared with Calidore, that catching sight of the graces tends instantly to dissipate them. Shakespeare's The Tempest gives unprecedented weight (in his age) to what Wordsworth was later to hail, in gratitude and wonder, as "Fallings from us, vanishings."[37] The Tempest magic produces

---

[37] William Wordsworth, "Ode: Intimations of Immortality from Recollections of Early Childhood," line 143, in Selected Poems and Prefaces, ed. Jack Stillinger (Boston: Houghton Mifflin, 1965).

28

fading illusions, dissolving shows that image more vividly than anything since Calidore's sighting of the Graces in The Faerie Queene, the fragile vision and discontinuous structure of romance:  yet when the magic finally dissolves, its intimations of a visionary world linger in our imagination.

Chapter II

"More than magic can perform": Greene and Peele

It was Aristotle who ruled that

> The story, as an imitation of an action, must
> represent one action, a complete whole, with its
> several incidents so closely connected that the
> transposal or withdrawal of any one of them will
> disjoin and dislocate the whole.[1]

And it is against Aristotelian standards that the twentieth century, no less than the sixteenth, defines the "multiple unity" of Elizabethan comedy.[2] My concern here, however, is less with dramatic unity than with the way two Elizabethans, Greene and Peele, negatively prove Aristotle's equation of imitation and coherent sequence. Progress in Friar Bacon and Friar Bungay and The Old Wives Tale is deliberately inconsequential throughout, even after allowing for textual corruption in The Old Wives Tale. Successive incidents or scenes are seldom bound in a relation of cause and effect;

---

[1] Aristotle, Poetics, viii. 1451a 30-34, tr. Ingram Bywater, with preface by Gilbert Murray (Oxford: Clarendon Press, 1954).

[2] Madeleine Doran, Endeavors of Art: A Study of Form in Elizabethan Drama (Madison: Univ. of Wisconsin Press, 1954), p. 6, quoting Wölfflin on Renaissance painting; I am indebted throughout to her excellent discussion of Aristotelian and Elizabethan unity especially pp. 273-340, and to that of Richard Levin, The Multiple Plot in English Renaissance Drama (Chicago: Univ. of Chicago Press, 1971), e.g. pp.1-20.

the continuity of visible physical realities on stage, and thus of time and space, is repeatedly broken. Both plays are consciously anti-mimetic, and, furthermore, governed not just by romance conventions but by the caprices of magicians. This chapter investigates the extent to which Greene and Peele justify structural discontinuity by the working of magic: this means studying the degree of control the magician exerts over the action of each play, and the steady decrease in his control as each play progresses. Elizabethan ambivalence about magic always imposed on the dramatist the duty to stage the collapse and/or repentance of the magician. Such debilitation of stage magic, itself built into the structure of these plays, undermines the principle of structural discontinuity on which magical stories are based. Under the Elizabethan scheme of things, a certain ritual skepticism about magically wrought miracles must preside over the happy resolution of the comedy, itself achieved by magic. The fact that no such shadow is cast over the endings of Friar Bacon and The Old Wives Tale despite the overt defeat of magic arts is evidence that Peele and Greene draw only a hesitant and incomplete analogy between the unrealism of their art, and the magic they dramatize. Artist is allowed a greater freedom and influence than his mirror image, the magician. The two plays therefore contain "more than magic can perform,"[3] and

[3] Greene, Friar Bacon, ed. D. Seltzer,ii.77; succeeding references to this play and Peele's are in my text.

31

Greene and Peele, I argue, do not control as fully as their contemporaries (Marlowe and Shakespeare) the instability that an ambiguously conceived magic may give to dramatic art.

"Magic's mystery," according to one of Friar Bacon's academic sidekicks, includes the use of prophecy "to plain out questions, as Apollo did" (ii.14-18). Like the oracles of Apollo, however, the magician's explanations raise as many questions as they answer. Bacon's easy superiority over temporal limitation, demonstrated not only by prophecies of an unrivalled opacity, but through the wilful illogic he superimposes on the history of his fellow characters, does little to pave our way into a demystified future: mystery is precisely magic's object. Bacon's magic is "prospective skill" (xiii.12) that attempts control over the future as much as simply foretelling. Bacon's efforts actually to remake the stories of other characters require a certain manipulation of space, and particularly of the bodies that occupy stage space. Magic, one of Bacon's devils confirms, traditionally involves the transcendence of geographical limitation:

> How restless are the ghosts of hellish spirits
> When every charmer with his magic spells
> Calls us from nine-fold trenched Phlegiton,
> To scud and over-scour the earth in post
> Upon the speedy wings of swiftest winds.
> Now Bacon hath rais'd me from the darkest deep
> To search about the world for Miles his man.
> (xv.1-7)

32

Friar Bacon's glass brings magic's conquest of space into sharp focus. As the editor of the Regents Renaissance Drama Series _Friar Bacon_, Daniel Seltzer, notes (v.105), "prospective" also implies, at least in this play, "perspective"; Bacon's glass conditions the immediate future by bridging distances.

The magician has already proved his ability to halt the movements and gestures of Warren, Ermsby, and Edward when he stills their drawn swords: in the glass scene that follows, he achieves an even more spectacular victory over space. Bacon and Edward, closeted in an Oxford study, view Fressingfield and the lovers in Bacon's magic glass. Friar Bungay is about to marry Margaret to Lacy. We do not have to take the visibility of Fressingfield on faith, for we too can see it (the actors are there in front of us). Nevertheless our faith is rigorously exercised as the scene develops. We are asked not to suspend our disbelief in the presence of the lovers but to disbelieve the evidence of our own eyes, to appreciate that the obviously solid actors playing the Fressingfield crew are in fact not "really" there. Yet more than our sense of sight and our commonsense are outraged by this proposition: we can _hear_ the alternation of conversations in Fressingfield and Oxford.[4]

---

[4] Robert H. West, _The Invisible World_, pp. 91-92, notes the usual Renaissance theory that people in magic glasses "were less in the glass than in the imaginations of the beholders," but points out that in Greene's source, Bacon's glass was a "perspective," that is, a scientifically exact reflector: he observes that the audience, unlike Edward, can

33

M.C. Bradbrook, writing on The Old Wives Tale, traces such liberties as the Elizabethans took with place and with strict narrative progression to the medieval dramatic convention of simultaneous stage setting.[5] This undeniable truth should however not lead us to overlook the thoughtfulness with which Greene reworks the convention. Greene has Bacon make magic nonsense of space, in order to set the mimetic and anti-mimetic purposes of playing in dramatic conflict with one another.

For the juxtaposition of the two locations on stage serves to subordinate one illusion to another -- yet Greene does not, finally, allow us to decide which "place" is more illusory. Bacon initially teaches Edward and us that Fressingfield is a mirage. He stops Edward from thrusting his sword in the glass. This, he says, would not help Edward, because the proximity of Fressingfield is an optical illusion:

> 'Twere a long poniard, my lord, to reach between
> Oxford and Fressingfield. (vi.131-32)

Edward excuses himself in terms more significant than he knows:

> Choler to see the traitors 'gree so well
> Made me think the shadows substances.

hear the Fressingfield conversation, but still concludes that Fressingfield is as illusory to us as to Edward.

[5] M.C.Bradbrook, "Peele's Old Wives' Tale: A Play of Enchantment," English Studies, 43 (1962), 323-25.

34

The glass prospective projects the sight but not the reality of Fressingfield to Oxford.

Yet the friar's envoy can cross over by magic into Fressingfield and halt events there. At the crucial moment in the wedding ceremony, Bacon stops Bungay's mouth and his servant-devil walks into Bungay's territory and carries him out of it. Bacon's magic, then, operates not just _by_ illusion (that is, by showing the lovers in the glass) but also _on_ illusions (changing, and breaking up, the Fressingfield picture). But the Fressingfield folk acquire more substantiality for us than Bacon is prepared to admit. His minion actively participates in the wedding scene, physically present with the "insubstantial" lovers, or, to put it another way, becomes, like the lovers and Bungay, one of the shadowy illusions we and Edward can see in the glass, which have, in actual fact, all the substance of real actors that our powers of cognition lead us to surmise. This is precisely the kind of juggling with illusion and reality of which Shakespeare was to become grand master, but at which Greene is not quite successful. It is not clear, for example, whether we actually see Fressingfield from the same direction as Edward does, and the choice might alter the meaning of the scene. The scene is not fully worked out: Greene's implied comparison between his own and Bacon's authorship of events, between the illusions of art and magic, breaks down. The figures of Bungay and the lovers

are simultaneously real and illusory, as actors both are
and are not the thing they represent; but, because the
subordination of illusory insubstantial Fressingfield
to "real" and substantial Oxford is actually only
intermittent, the juxtaposition of the two places in
the scene does not make a consistent or sustained
metatheatrical statement.

The Lambert and Serlsby subplot confirms the potential of
the magic glass to conjure realities from immaterialities.
Lambert and Serlsby in Suffolk are visible in Oxford through
the glass. The witnesses, the student sons, are good
friends like their fathers. The fathers' duel propels the
sons into mortal combat. Again, both groups are physically
present on stage, and can be heard in conversation, and,
again, the second place, here Suffolk, the area around
Fressingfield, has only a secondary substantiality. But the
sons mirror the actions of their fathers; reality imitates
illusion. If, in the wedding scene, Oxford temporarily
conditions the outcome of events in Fressingfield, here, at
least, Suffolk influences Oxford. Thus, once more, the
illusoriness of Suffolk is called into question. Greene
consistently makes illusions seem real and makes real
presences take on the qualities of the illusions juxtaposed
with them: the merely dramatic creations and their
magically induced counterparts are mutual reflections.
Nature at times appears briefly to imitate magic art.

36

Sometimes, however, Bacon's magic actually transports the substance as well as a picture of something from one site to another. The hostess of the Bell Inn at Henley, who is whisked to Oxford by the magician, has no idea of how she has got there: she participates in the Oxford scene more substantially than do the lovers, Bungay, or Lambert and Serlsby. Here Bacon's magic actually displaces the body. Bacon doubly exploits the frailties of the flesh which is, here, moved as easily by magic as it is by concupiscence. He removes the Hostess to Oxford to show the shaky foundation on which Burden's academic reputation rests: Burden's "book" of alchemy is, in actual fact, not a book but the less esoteric charms of the Hostess, and his magic is merely one of the commoner sins that flesh is heir to. Miles echoes this connection of lust with magic when he tells Bacon: "I'll warrant you, master, if Master Burden could conjure as well as you, he would have his book every night from Henley to study on at Oxford (ii.146-48): Greene's intention to cast an ironic reflection on Bacon's lust (for power rather than women) at this point is unremarked in the play's dialogue or action.

Magic in Friar Bacon is usually as pointlessly destructive as it is here. Bacon claims he has power to raise tempests and disorder the seasons, though we never see him doing such things. Even the images of permanence he promises for England are emblems of mutability, associated

37

with corrupt and doomed civilzations, brazen rather than
golden worlds:

> I have contriv'd and fram'd a head of brass
> (I made Belcephon hammer out the stuff),
> And that by art shall read philosophy;
> And I will strengthen England by my skill,
> That if ten Caesars liv'd and reign'd in Rome,
> With all the legions Europe doth contain,
> They should not touch a grass of English ground.
> The work that Ninus rear'd at Babylon,
> The brazen walls fram'd by Semiramis,
> Carved out like to the portal of the sun,
> Shall not be such as rings the English strond
> From Dover to the market place of Rye.(ii.55-66)

We suspect from the start that the wall of brass will never
materialize, for as constituted it cannot possibly realize
Bacon's dreams of grandeur and fame.  Bacon's magic more
often destroys such illusions as are wrought by others than
it conjures up his own.  The friar establishes his supremacy
over the rival magician Vandermast by breaking up and then
banishing both Vandermast and his shows.  Bungay, aiming to
prove his grasp of

> strange necromantic spells
> That work such shows and wondering in the world
> (ix.47-48)

has conjured a tree with a fire-shooting dragon sitting on
it, and Vandermast replies by producing a Hercules to
destroy the tree and unseat the dragon.  These shows, like
the visions in Bacon's glass, are shadows, not substantial
bodies; the Hercules is rather a "fiend appearing like great
Hercules" (99).  Vandermast loses the contest because Bacon
orders a spirit to "vanish the tree and thou away with him"
(161).  Once again, Bacon does not catch the latent warning

of his own magic's fragility. By the end of the play, when a devil carries Bacon's apprentice Miles to hell on his back (recalling Bacon's transportation of Bungay and the hostess), Greene is to Bacon what Bacon is to lesser magicians.

Bacon's real moment of defeat comes before the duel scene, when the Brazen Head finally materializes. Bacon's labors are all lost in bathos, as the Head announces that "Time is ... Time was ... Time is past" (xi.53,65,75). Miles, understandably unable to discern in this the signal of great things to come, fails to wake his master in time: on this sin of omission hinges the turning point of Bacon's career both as magician and as controller of the dramatic action. The friar reads more into the situation than we can: his furious inquisition of Miles is funny not just because Bacon has slept through his great moment, but because the greatness of the moment is called into question. The magician's reaction to Miles' disclosure invests the time just past with a significance never fully explained. Bacon obviously regards the Head as considerably more than a speaking clock; it will, he says, utter strange and uncouth aphorisms and gird England with that inscrutably valuable wall of brass. How or why the Head should do these things remains a mystery, and Bacon does nothing to demystify us. The magician has suspended time, and now does time suspend him; his own engine, defeating him, promptly self-destructs, vanishes out of sight. What Greene dramatizes in this disappearing act is the real vacuity at the heart of the magician's endeavor. The Head, while on stage, makes negative capital on the idea of the dramatic moment, delivering with sound and fury what actually signifies nothing.

Bacon finally admits that his magic shows are as fragile as Vandermast's and Bungay's, and cannot legitimately claim the privilege of permanence. After the double duel scene of Lamberts and Serlsbys, Bacon suddenly gives vent to lamentation and repentance:

> This glass prospective worketh many woes;
> And therefore, seeing these brave, lusty brutes,
> These friendly youths did perish by thine art,
> End all thy magic and tine art at once.
> The poniard that did end the fatal lives
> Shall break the cause efficiat of their woes.
> So fade the glass, and end with it the shows
> That nigromancy did infuse the crystal with.
> (xiii.76-84)

Thus Bacon does what he prevented Edward from doing earlier, stabbing the glass. The magic that works the insubstantial shows does not "Eternize Friar Bacon for his art" (ii.43); his shows are all fading pageants, and his interference with the realities of time and space does not effect the play's final and major transformations (the reconciliation of unharmonious elements into a newly coherent social unity).

The truest magic is contained in other transforming agencies. When the repentant magician turns back to religion, Margaret, the play's moral center, turns from the religious life she has planned and yields to the enchantment of genuine love:

40

> The flesh is frail.  My lord dothe know it well,
> That when he comes with his enchanting face,
> Whatso'er betide, I cannot say him nay.
>                     (xiv.86-88)

But love transcends the sins of the flesh, which, as we
have seen, include magic.  Lacy tells Margaret how, when
he saw her,

> Love, like a wag, straight dived into my heart,
> And there did shrine the idea of yourself.
>                     (vi.79-80)

Seltzer glosses idea, appropriately, as image, but the
Platonic echo is also unmistakable.  Love can do more than
magic can perform, creating ideal situations where magic
merely distorts realities.  Margaret's status is raised by
her response to Lacy's unforgiveable test of her virture,
"from her homely cottage to the court" (xvi.20).  Greene
makes haste to transform the court into a suitable
destination for the fair maid of Fressingfield:  and gives
the job of singing England's praises to the unfrocked
magician.

Bacon finds "by deep prescience" of his art that
England's future is securer than it could ever have been
made by his magic wall of brass.  This is the only evidence
in the play that magic per se might have the idealizing
power of love or poetry.  But Bacon's prophecy here is
only tangentially or metaphorically magical; it is not
radically different from standard poetic expressions of
England's ideal destiny.  Greene's concept of dramatic
transforming magic is subsumed in, and less than, the

41

poetic convention.[6] Bacon is now only foretelling the future, not creating it, responding to and not engineering the miraculous changes Greene has worked in the hearts of the court. This, finally, is the poetic answer to the brazenness of nature and of Bacon's earlier magic:

> here where Brute did build his Troynovant,
> From forth the royal garden of a king
> Shall flourish out so rich and fair a bud
> Whose brightness shall deface proud Phoebus'
> flower,
> And over-shadow Albion with her leaves.
> Till then Mars shall be master of the field;
> But then the stormy threats of wars shall cease.
> The horse shall stamp as careless of the pike;
> Drums shall be turn'd to timbrels of delight;
> With wealthy favors plenty shall enrich
> The strond that gladded wand'ring Brute to see,
> And peace from heaven shall harbor in these leaves
> That gorgeous beautifies this matchless flower.
> Apollo's hellitropian then shall stoop,
> And Venus' hyacinth shall vail her top;
> Juno shall shut her gillyflowers up,
> And Pallas' bay shall bask her brightest green;
> Ceres' carnation, in consort with those,
> Shall stoop and wonder at Diana's rose.
> (xvi.44-62)

England, in short, is and will be defended far more surely by "the walls of old Oceanus" and by clean living, by observation of the golden rule, than by more magic and brazen encirclements. The change in England by the play's end is reflected in the changed language of her king.

---

[6] See e.g. George Peele, The Araygnment of Paris, ed. R. Mark Benbow, in vol.3, The Life and Works of George Peele, ed. C. Prouty, 1138-75, in which Englanders "are ycleeped Angeli"; and W. Shakespeare, King Henry VIII, New Arden ed. R.A. Foakes (London: Methuen, 1957), V.iv.17-55, Cranmer's prophecy of Elizabethan England's greatness: it is interesting that the King's reply, "Thou speakest wonders," (55) suggests the magical quality of such poetry.

42

Bacon's blueprint for a brazen wall like that round Babylon is recalled in Henry's early description of the waters about Europe, which are

> like the battlements
> That compass'd high-built Babel in with towers.
> (iv.3-4)

But by the end, after Bacon's prophecy, Henry compares England's moat to the rivers of paradise, "Gihon and swift Euphrates" (xvi.66). Poetic and romantic idealization accomplish more than merely magical transformations can, and brazen magic is translated in golden art.

Greene's play admits only the ambitions of magic that can be brought into line with substitutes for magic. Mason cites magic's potential "to work/Wonders that pass the common sense of men" (ii.74-75), but, immediately, Greene ironizes what Shakespeare will, in his plays of magic, justify:

> But Bacon roves a bow beyond his reach,
> And tells of more than magic can perform,
> Thinking to get a fame by fooleries.(ii.76-78)

Bacon, like Marlowe's Faustus, fails by over-extending himself, straining beyond nature. Greene, on the brink of equating magic with his imaginative art of constructive unrealism, rules finally for renunciation and against over-reaching. Bacon's magic is, predominantly, evil, and only his repentance purchases for him what Edward wins by relinquishing another illicit desire:

43

>So in subduing fancy's passion,
>Conquering thyself, thou get'st the richest spoil.
>                                    (viii.120-21)

If the language of this suggests a still-insufficient piety,
it is nonetheless a more sophisticated expression of
ambition's dangers than anything in The Old Wives Tale;
Peele's magic is of another sort.


The discontinuities of The Old Wives Tale are at first
sight more difficult to disentangle than those of Friar
Bacon, partly because the greater confusion of sequence may
owe something to a corrupt text. The brevity of the play
has led some scholars such as Harold Jenkins to argue that
the extant text is an abridged or mutilated version of the
original. Even Jenkins however concedes that one of the
primary factors in the play's surface incoherence is
probably the rambling narrative of the old wife, and that
"the inconsequentiality of the whole action as it would
shape itself in Madge's imagination ... is the result of
conscious art."[7] Madge adds elements to her narration out of
sequence; she forgets some strands of her plot and leaves
others only vaguely sketched. Her story opens indefinitely:

[7] Harold Jenkins, "Peele's 'Old Wive's Tale'," MLR, 34
(1939), 180; see also his discussion 177-85; also
P.H.Cheffaud, George Peele, (Paris: Librairie Felix Alcan,
1913), pp. 114-16.

44

> Once uppon a time there was a King or a Lord, or a
> Duke that had a faire daughter, the fairest that
> ever was; as white as snowe, and as redd as bloud:
> and once upon a time his daughter was stollen away,
> and he sent all his men to seeke out his daughter,
> and hee sent so long, that he sent all his men out
> of his Land. (110-15)

Now, having begun (once upon a time) twice, and having

anticipated the near-end of the tale (the loss of all the

kingdom's men), she retraces her steps abruptly, filling in a

key detail (the kidnapper's identify), but in so doing, finds

herself unable to avoid repeating the whole story, this time

with embellishments:

> O Lord I quite forgot, there was a Conjurer, and
> this Conjurer could doo anything, and hee turned
> himselfe into a great Dragon, and carried the
> Kinges Daughter away in his mouth to a Castle that
> hee made of stone, and there he kept hir I know not
> how long, till at last all the Kinges men went out
> so long, that hir two Brothers went to seeke hir.
> O I forget: she (he I would say) turned a proper
> yong man to a Beare in the night, and a man in the
> day, and keeps by a crosse that parts three
> severall waies, and he made his Lady run mad: gods
> me bones, who comes here? (119-28)

Madge's narrative difficulties stem from her subject

matter as much as from the mingle-mangle of her mind: it is

next to impossible to relate in orderly fashion a complex

set of simultaneous quests after a single maiden. The

obstreperousness of Madge's raw material quickly makes

itself felt: the maiden's two brothers materialize in full

view of Madge and her on-stage audience, preempting her

45

tale-telling efforts. As Frolic points out: "Soft Gammer, here some come to tell your tale for you" (130). Madge thereafter makes only occasional contributions, most of which are supernumerary and useless: for example she only thinks to tell us that Lampriscus "was a begar, and dwelt uppon a greene" (249) after Lampriscus has left.

But as the characters enter one by one, our sense of spatial distortion and temporal disturbance actually increases. The relationship of the various characters is so confusing that I present a summary here, before going on to examine the nature of the collective entanglement. Delia, the king's daughter abducted by the magician Sacrapant, is sought by two unnamed brothers and two suitors, Huanebango and Corebus. These two suitors are in the end matched to Lampriscus' two daughters, Zantippa and Celanta. Erestus, the young man at the crossroads who is turned by Sacrapant into an old man by day and a bear by night, is the betrothed husband of the mad Venelia who wanders distractedly through the play. Her male correlative is Eumenides, the wandering knight in love with Delia, and in the end, Delia's successful suitor. The dead and unburied parishoner Jack, who seems at first irrelevant, turns out in the end to be the instrument of Sacrapant's defeat (or at least one of the instruments). Like Huanebango, he is resurrected from the dead.

The unbridled energy of Peele's plotting may not represent successful art, but it does seem to reflect the conscious exercise of genuine talent. As in _Friar Bacon_, the discontinuities of the dramatic action, which would be glaringly evident even were we presented only with the rapid entrances and exits of Peele's several relatively undifferentiated characters, are brought into especial prominence, and made to seem magical, by the fact that characters frequently materialize upon being mentioned in the narrative, and swiftly vanish into thin air. Venelia, like the two brothers, enters briefly when her name is mentioned (Erestus, not Madge, is the narrator at this point). Sometimes narrative mention follows physical presence, as when (248-49) Madge announces the entry of those curiously functionless harvest men. Perhaps their brief appearances, so completely divorced from any of the play's plot strands, represent something left out of the text: as the text now stands, however, their effect is almost surreal, suggesting perhaps other unseen presences who contemplate the play's action from some vantage point off-stage. This is the kind of speculation that the play's worst eccentricities encourage and frustrate in the audience. The rapid materializing and vanishing of shapes on stage, often accomplished without explanation of any kind, unsettles our faith in either their solidity or permanence, and undermines the art's illusions by enhancing, not diminishing, our sense of wonder.

47

Some of the capriciousness of dialogue and story is clearly the result either of textual omission or of the folkloric tonality of their presentation. When Erestus asks the two brothers "Was shee fayre?" (154) before he is supposed to know that she (Delia) is the object of their quest, we realize that either something has been dropped or that Peele simply lost grip on the sequence of events.[8] When Erestus spontaneously gives Lampriscus a detailed set of instructions for the rehabilitation into society of his two daughters, we hear the overtones of folktale: "send them to the Well for the Water of life: there shall they find their fortunes unlooked for" (238-39), and we accept the genesis of this new story line without remark or difficulty.

But other communication between mutually unintroduced characters is established with little preparation or justification, and often a clumsiness that seem independent of textual inadequacies. Eumenides, advised by Erestus to "dreame of no rest" (447), almost immediately awakes (479) to prevent violence between Wiggen and the sexton over the burial money of Jack. The absence of any stage direction to indicate Eumenides' falling asleep is probably a function of the mutilated text, but the hastiness with which Eumenides is brought into companionship with Jack represents artistic as opposed to textual failure. Yet many other quick changes and instant developments of plot are patently authoritative

[8] Frank S. Hook, ed., note to 154.

and artisticlly compelling. A recurring feature of the Eumenides-Jack association is temporal reversal. Jack is resurrected from the dead when Eumenides offers to pay for his burial; Eumenides' almost empty purse is magically refilled at the Inn. This standard temporal reversal of folktale is beautifully enriched by Peele as the men approach the Inn: Jack, until now the follower of Eumenides, goes ahead of him to the Inn to bespeak a meal, and the roles of follower and leader are exchanged. This provides a visible sign of Jack's impending dominance in the action: it is as though Peele anticipates, for us, Jack's seizure of initiatives from Eumenides and even more importantly, from Sacrapant.

The part played by the magician in the temporal and spatial oddities of the play's action is not as substantial as the author's -- Peele gives less to the magician than Greene does. Sacrapant's magic, like Peele's, involves according to him summoning up, dismissing, and changing the "shapes of mortall men" (343). He has enormous control over the physical presences he wants on stage. He can conjure meat from England and wine from France to the lady (Delia) he has imprisoned. When Delia's two brothers arrive he is quick to whisk Delia off-stage; Peele gives to this exit a miraculous quality through the words of the first brother, "Or was it but her shadow that was here?" (394). But Peele does not, any where in this play, develop as fully as Greene

the common illusoriness of magic and dramatic shows: here
Sacrapant's seizure of Delia from her brothers, repeating
the earlier abduction, is not a truly magic disappearing act
but a simple stage exit, and the potential meditation on
magical drama in the brother's remark goes unrealized.
There is admittedly much magic in Sacrapant's habitual
removal of intrusive bodies from center stage: he reenters
when the two brothers are on the point of drawing swords,
and, amid thunder and lightning, gets two of his furies to
carry the brothers off to his cell. Sacrapant's control of
physical appearance is of a cruder and less objective type
than Bacon's, since his primary illusion is not the
conjuring of other physical presences but the clothing of
his old body in a youthful shape that does not belong to
him. Sacrapant's most stunning victory over material
realities, time and space, is the prolongation of his own
life by the light in the glass hidden under a turf: "With
this inchantment I do anything./And till this fades, my
skill shall still endure" (426-27).

If Sacrapant's magic sustains his own life, it interrupts
the progress of others': it is because of Sacrapant's
influence that Huanebango is struck down (Huanebango is
seeking Sacrapant to wrest Delia from him) to the
accompaniment of "A voice and flame of fire." Even such
apocalyptic moments, like most of the magically-wrought
discontinuities in the action, are more usually simply
breaks or direction changes in the action than the shape

50

changes that Sacrapant identifies as his magic's primary function: this magic works more often negatively than positively. In this case, Sacrapant's furies carry Huanebango off to open fields for the scavengers: he is, presumably, dead. Corebus, Huanebango's companion, is merely struck blind, a condition not dissimilar to Delia's, when she is made unable to recognize her brothers.

But the magician here overplays his hand. Merely protecting Delia from the knowledge of her own identity and desirability does not guarantee Sacrapant's success as he hopes it will. She is still quite visible. And though she loyally covers up Sacrapant's all-important light under the hill from the prying eyes of her brothers, the odds against Sacrapant rapidly lengthen during the scene. Rather than banish the brothers, which would seem the safest course for a magician as incompetent as Sacrapant, he sets them to work as country slaves to "worke and dig for gold" (576) on "this inchaunted ground" (570). Magicians in Tudor England were often employed to help in digging for treasure; here, however, the normal order is reversed as the magician employs the diggers. Sacrapant furthermore sets the brothers to dig perilously close to the light in the glass, under the hill, the light that sustains his life. The brothers are coerced to play the role of "hill-diggers," the name given in the England of the time to those who wanted to get rich quickly:

See Keith Thomas, Religion and the Decline of Magic, pp. 279-80, on magicians and "hill-diggers" in Tudor England.

51

the treasure for which the brothers are set to dig turns out to be the death of the magician. Control of the action is clearly slipping away from Sacrapant.

The next scene suggests an alternative authority within the play's cast. Zantippa and Celanta, the respectively scolding and ugly daughters of Lampriscus, enter at the well of life, where the two girls have come with pitchers to get some of the water of life. This is more or less delicately linked to the acquiring of a husband: "Belike husbands grow by the Well side." They have come, though, not at the bidding or under the influence of Sacrapant, but at the advice of Erestus, the man at the crossroads. It is easy to overlook this point, as, in the middle of the scene, Sacrapant's indefatiguable furies take advantage of a brief absence of the daughters to produce Huanebango out of Sacrapant's cell and drag him toward the well of life. In fact, however, the cell and well are one and the same place, as is suggested by the stage direction at 630: "Enter two Furies out of the Conjurers Cell and laies Huanebango by the well of life. Enter Zantippa with a Pitcher to the Well." When Zantippa reenters and tries to dip her pitcher into the well, a head speaks inside it, and when she breaks her pitcher over it (Peele seems determined to anticipate Freud), Huanebango arises from the dead. It is unclear whether his resuscitation is achieved by Sacrapant or by

52

Zantippa's action, initiated by the counsel of Erestus; the other resurrection in the play, Jack's, is not the work of Sacrapant, but his author. Yet Huanebango's presence, and the convenient deafness which will preserve his sanity when married to the scold Zantippa, are the products of Sacrapant's magic. Sacrapant and Erestus, the magician and his victim, seem to share the responsibility for the marriage of Huanebango and Zantippa. Why the magician should help the lovers is never explained; Sacrapant has already got rid of Huanebango's threat to his possession of Delia by arranging Huanebango's death. But if the lack of clarification here seems a weakness in the play's construction, this new juxtaposition of Erestus and Sacrapant as central powers over the play's action is not: in fact it is a brilliant piece of engineering on Peele's part.

The play gradually pushes into prominence the undeclared competition between Erestus and Sacrapant for the central position in the play's structure. As always in this play the question of centrality is posed initially in terms of geographical location. Erestus, at the beginning of the play, occupies the physical center of action, the crossroads at which three ways meet and by which almost everyone passes. As Madeleine Doran has observed, this creates a radial effect[10] that physically images and justifies the

[10] Doran, Endeavors of Art, p.301.

53

web-like structure of the play's interlocking stories. At
the center, then, of all the paths traced by the characters,
is Erestus. But all the roads lead to Sacrapant: since most
of the characters are seeking Delia, most are perforce
making their way deliberately to the magician. It is
curious, and in retrospect, ironic, that Erestus' central
position is one of bondage rather than liberty and power.
The real center of influence in the early part of the action
is located at the end of the road, not in the geographical
center at all. Sacrapant's position at the periphery of the
radial structure, which at first magically encloses the
circular action, becomes, in the end, an image of his
vulnerability. For the concerted ambitions of all the
characters are to rob him of his power to draw them to him
(Delia). The pursuit of this Beauty requires one who "can
monsters tame, laboures atchive, riddles absolve, loose
inchantments, murther magicke, and kill conjuring" (268-71).
Sacrapant's magic turns out to mean his annihilation: his
magician's power to sustain his own life is limited by the
power of that self-same magic to attract his enemies and his
destroyers. Magic, the means of his dominance, becomes, in
circular fashion, the instrument of his defeat.

When Huanebango and Booby pass the crossroads they ask
Erestus how to get to Sacrapant. Erestus' oracular
description of Sacrapant's whereabouts as "Faire inough, and
farr inough from thy fingering sonne" (i.e. Booby, 306-307)

is, like his advice to Lampriscus, an early hint of his future importance as counterweight to the magician. Erestus is always mysterious: his prophecies tend to leave us, like Eumenides, in a "Laborinth" (439-48). Though Erestus frequently displays the gift of prophecy (330-32), the rivalry for prominence which Peele establishes between Erestus and Sacrapant is not a competition between magicians. Erestus in fact is never conscious of his influence or his threat to that of the magician. The mirror relationship of reverse reflection between Sacrapant and Erestus is felt only by Sacrapant. He tells us that he stole Delia

> to revive the man,
> That seemeth yong and pleasant to behold,
> And yet is aged, crooked, weake and numbe.
> Thus by inchaunting spells I doo deceive,
> Those that behold and looke upon my face;
> But well I may bid youthfull years adue.(347-51)

And Delia describes Sacrapant as "this faire yong man" (584-85). Sacrapant's youth is as illusory as Erestus' old age. It is not until the end of the play that we discover that this is more than a neat juxtaposition of illusions: Sacrapant, we learn from Jack, actually "tooke the shape of the olde man that kept the cross, and that old man was in the likeness of the Conjurer." This statement, though confused, indicates that Sacrapant's youthful shape is Erestus' true form, and that Erestus' aged appearance is precisely that of the magician. Or, in simpler terms, we might say that Sacrapant's soul is concealed in Erestus' body, and Erestus' soul by Sacrapant's body.

Peele's structural achievement in The Old Wives Tale is of considerable sophistication, and the greatest argument for the play's conscious artistry. All the roads that lead to the magician are the roads that lead to the destruction of magic, and, in a curious way, to Erestus. Erestus' early central postion at the crossroads becomes, in the ending, a forecast of his eventual supremacy over Sacrapant. Erestus, released from servitude by the destruction of the magician, makes his way to the circumference of the circle, and the center and outermost limits of the radial structure appear to fuse. This is of course visibly evident more on stage than page, since the two "places" are on the same ground, and the wandering characters do not, at least visibly, ever put much distance between the crossroads and the cell or well. Peele undermines the magic of Sacrapant by a strategy of inexact duplication: the duality of magic, at once the means of miracles and the engine of its own collapse, is given visual shape in the persons of Erestus and Sacrapant, and the places associated with them. Erestus, never a magician, is nonetheless the reverse image, the reflection and antithesis of the enchanter; the lines between Erestus and Sacrapant are drawn very tight.

The play suffers, however, from Peele's obsession with doubleness. The other obvious analogies between plot strands are not sufficiently developed to clarify our impressions as analogous actions often do in other multiple plot dramas. The play's curious near-repetitions increase the difficulty we experience in keeping a grip on events. The proliferation of stories that are almost identical, such as the histories of Jack and Huanebango, Eumenides and Erestus, Venelia and Delia (whose wits are removed by the magician late in the play), prevents either clear contrast or easy comparison. Joan C. Marx notes acutely "Peele's fascination with replaying language and gesture with slight variation of form":[11] the play, like Madge's story, is not clarified by its habitual repetition with embellishment. Indeed the wealth of comparison imposes an additional burden on the audience by demanding not just tolerance but comprehension of its intricacies.

Erestus is not, for example, Sacrapant's only partial double or alter ego, and the alternatives to Erestus are not all equally convincing counterweights to the magician. Eumenides, the wandering knight seeking an imprisoned lady, is the reverse reflection of Erestus, the man confined at the crossroads, and sought by a wandering lady, Venelia. This, if we submit to the play's flexible comparative method, brings Eumenides into a closer relationship with Sacrapant than merely that of rival suitor for the hand of

---

[11] Joan C. Marx, "'Soft, Who Have We Here?': The Dramatic Technique of The Old Wives Tale," Renaissance Drama, n.s. 12 (1981), 139.

57

Delia: if Eumenides is the reverse image of Erestus then he ought to share something of Sacrapant's identity, especially given the general lack of differentiation among characters in Peele's play. But since Eumenides is innocent both in deed and in name, and since he gets Delia only when Sacrapant loses her, he is hardly a real parallel.

A better reverse image to Sacrapant is provided in the person of Jack, who acts rather like a benevolent magician, and whose history in the play, from death to resurrected life to death again, resembles Sacrapant's living on borrowed time. Sacrapant staves off his death by magical means; Peele magically allows Jack a mandate to come back from the dead long enough to confound the magician. Jack's several feats include stopping up Eumenides' ears so he "shall not be intised with [Sacrapant's] inchanting speeches" (795). Sacrapant here becomes a siren figure; elsewhere, though, he too induces deafness -- on Huanebango, the other figure resurrected from the dead. There is a set of incompletely realized parallels here: Jack, already like Huanebango, now acts like the magician, but the implicit comparison of the deafened Eumenides with the deaf Huanebango serves no corresponding purpose, and seems an accidental corollary of the primary analogy between Jack and Sacrapant rather than a deliberate strategy. And when Jack kills Sacrapant he is invisible to Eumenides, having the power, like the magician, to induce blindness (as Sacrapant did upon Huanebango's companion, Corebus or Booby).

Furthermore these indications of Jack's semi-magical powers are not confirmed in Jack's most substantive action, at the end of the play: his defeat of the magician and his explanation of Sacrapant's career are not imaged as magical actions. Peele's presentation of Jack is unsatisfying, and his resolution of the main plot is weakened by giving a Johnny-come-lately the key role. The substitution of Jack for Erestus as Sacrapant's chief opposition is made so late that the tightness of the play's admirably conceived radial structure is jeopardized. Erestus has propelled most of the characters to Sacrapant, but it is Jack who gets the job of unravelling the play's mysteries. And in fact the explications of magic offered by Jack only substantiate what we have already been told by Sacrapant: "without this [the light] the Conjurer could do nothing, and so long as this light lasts, so long doth his arte indure, and this being out, then doth his arte decay" (827-29). Peele's conclusion destroys what coherence his dramatic structure achieves: typical of this weakening economy (and indicating possible textual corruption) is the presentation of two deaths for Sacrapant, one engineered by Jack, and one by Venelia, who breaks the glass and blows out the light.

Peele's play contains an unresolved conflict between rival structural principles. The author's own magic, congruent and superior to that of his magician Sacrapant, "explains" or rationalizes dramatic discontinuity, the strange materializing and vanishing of characters on stage, and the violations of spatial and temporal logic required to propel the plots to their miraculously happy conclusion. Yet the need Peele apparently felt to overthrow the magician in the ending leads him to adopt an alternative structural strategy, in which he emphasizes parallels to Sacrapant, characters whose influence is first juxtaposed with and finally preferred to the magician's force to effect change. Neither the discontinuities of sequence nor the mirror plotting quite cancel each other out; the demolition of the magic is as hasty and incomplete as is its establishment as the means of dramatic transformation and resolution. Peele's play is a less searching and less conscious exploration of illusion than Greene's; yet for all that, and for all the failures of textual transmission, The Old Wives Tale is strangely compelling.

Peele's play, like Friar Bacon and Friar Bungay, contains more than its explicitly dramatized magic can perform. Each magician fails and cedes his power to some other influence within the play: Friar Bacon loses ground to the transforming power of love and poetry, and Sacrapant, more simply, to the growing dominance of alternative characters. Such conflicting estimates of the value of magic as were current in England during the 1580s and 90s doubtless lie behind the double portrayal of the magician in Greene and

Peele. It is less clear why they damaged their own self-portraits as artists by identifying with a figure to which the popular imagination attached such dubiousness, or why, having decided on the identification, the artists did not draw its limits with more clarity. Their magicians are catalysts in the dramatic development, controllers of the discontinuities of marvellous and comedic action. But the restriction of the magician's operations, and his final discrediting in turn undermine the the artistic achievement of his author. Amid the profuseness and energy of these two plays we discern authorial indecisiveness in the portrayal of the magician. The analogy between artist and magician is incompletely presented. Sacrapant and Friar Bacon use many of their authors' strategies to effect wonderful changes, yet are never easily identified with real controllers of dramatic progress. The salutary transformations of each play's ending are contingent on the separation of artist and magician, the disenchantment, as it were, of an artistic method inherently magical: but there is no internal dramatic recognition of the paradox. Thus Greene's and Peele's labors seem to confute themselves, just as the labors of their magicians tend to self-destruct. The next chapter, on _Doctor Faustus_, presents Marlowe's more provocative and comprehensive exploration of contemporary inhibitions about magic. In _Doctor Faustus_ the ties that bind artist with magician are stronger, and the man of imagination more closely identified with the magician. Here too the force propelling magic and imagination leads ultimately to its own dissolution, but here, uniquely, the defeat of over-reaching fantasies is conceived in tragic terms.

# Chapter III

## Over-reaching fantasies:  Marlovian magic

A study of structural discontinuities in Marlowe's _Doctor Faustus_ faces an initial textual hurdle even more worrying than that of _The Old Wives Tale_:  the A-text and B-text are each fractured and faulty, and each bear some smatch of authority.  Thus, as Michael Warren notes in a recent article:

> the compilation or distillation of a single text of any value, let alone authority, from the totality of what is available to us _is not_ possible.  The extent of our knowledge and the immensity of our ignorance about the history of _Doctor Faustus_ renders the pursuit of a single composite text for interpretation or performance futile and rash ... historical knowledge or surmise about the text's 'quality' is not separable from interpretation of the text itself, and ... judgments of 'quality' in circumstances such as those surrounding _Doctor Faustus_ are not independent of considerations of meaning and performance.[1]

Warren's argument against conflating the texts, though unattractive to critics desiring a firm underpinning of their readings, is logically indisputable.  However it is easier to restrict oneself to only one of Marlowe's texts than it would be to exclude one of the _Lear_ or _Hamlet_ texts.

---

[1] Michael J.Warren, "_Doctor Faustus_:  The Old Man and the Text," _ELR_, 11.2 (1981), 115.

63

The B-text,[2] having fewer "holes" that unequivocally reflect errors in textual transmission, is better adapted to my purposes: at least if my analysis of structural gaps intended by Marlowe is occasionally vitiated by textual corruption, something of it may stand by default, since corruption in the B-text is more a question of uncanonical additions than the subtractions of the  printing-house, which are arguably even more capricious.[3]

For however difficult it is to be sure that any given break in our text was of Marlowe's creating, we cannot escape the conclusion that the play is structured as a series of only loosely connected episodes, and that some incoherence is in part contrived.  It is this deliberate variation on logical sequence as much as the preoccupation of the central character that connect Marlowe's tragedy  to the magical comedy of Greene and Peele, Marlowe's fellow University Wits.  The overall design of Doctor Faustus, even more than that of Friar Bacon and The Old Wives Tale, is a free-ranging movement through far-flung places and times, from Faustus' study to Rome, to Germany, and back to his study.  Faustus' roving disposition, expressed initially in his restless experimentation with various fields of

---

[2] W.W. Greg, ed., Marlowe's Doctor Faustus, 1604-1616: Parallel Texts (Oxford: Clarendon Press, 1950):I use Greg's conjectural reconstruction of the B-text throughout, and his through-line numbering (with act and scene divisions retained for the sake of convenience), and succeeding references to it are in my text.

[3] See Warren's excellent discussion, cited above.

64

endeavor, leads him logically to that art which, he tells us, gives a man in his study the freedom of the world. Magic lends its practitioner a power that "Stretcheth as farre as doth the mind of man" (I.i.87): the magician can travel through any time and space he likes without regard to physical limitations, as easily as his mind jumps from one subject to another in his unceasing drive for personal power. This chapter examines the extent to which the discontinuous movement of the drama through time and space reflects the overreaching imaginative fantasies Faustus entertains and indulges from one moment to the next. I investigate the degree to which Faustus' art, magic, is identified with his own imagination and the imaginative impulses of his author.[4] At the beginning of the play and through its course magic and imagination are posited as similar forces, thrusting beyond the normal restrictions of time and space, and the familiar barriers between flesh and spirit, reality and illusion. Faustus, like Marlowe,

[4] Critics of Marlowe and this play tend to divide according to their estimate of the degree of identification between playwright and his damned magician-hero: of those who find close sympathy between the two the most influential is perhaps Harry Levin, The Overreacher: A Study of Christopher Marlowe (Cambridge: Harvard Univ. Press, 1952), pp. 108-35; of those who assert Marlowe's theological and moral orthodoxy and thus his censure of Faustus two representative examples are Charles G. Masinton, Christopher Marlowe's Tragic Vision (Athens: Ohio Univ. Press, 1972), pp. 113-42, and W.L. Godshalk, The Marlovian World Picture (The Hague: Mouton, 1974), pp. 169-203; those who see a partial identification and sympathy between Marlowe and his magician and who find in the play, as I do, an unresolved contradiction include J.B. Steane, Marlowe: A Critical Study (Cambridge: The Univ. Press, 1964), pp. 154-65.

65

summons up illusions, unreal imitations of substance, that is, puts on magic shows. Yet all these overreaching efforts swiftly dissolve: by the conclusion of the play the leveller "at the end of every art," Faustus the magician-playwright, discovers that magic inevitably collapses in "idle fantasies,/ To over-reach the Divell" (V.ii./1909-10). The conclusion of the chapter discusses the relationship between Faustus' damnation and Marlowe's estimate of imaginative art, and argues that Marlowe, by simultaneously underwriting and denigrating the overreaching fantasies of magicians and artists, confirms the unresolvable contradictions at which Greene and Peele only hint, and which make Marlowe's play great tragedy.

Faustus' early paean to his chosen profession draws a striking comparison between magic and art:

> O what a world of profite and delight,
> Of power, of honour, and omnipotence,
> Is promised to the Studious Artizan?
> All things that moue between the quiet Poles
> Shall be at my command: Emperors and Kings,
> Are but obey'd in their severall Prouinces:
> But his dominion that exceeds in this,
> Stretcheth as farre as doth the mind of man:
> A sound Magitian is a Demi-god
> Here tire my braines to get a Deity. (I.i.80-89)

The profit and delight for which Faustus lusts recollect and yet distinguish themselves from the more innocent ambitions of Sidney's poet to teach and delight:[5] acquisitiveness has

---

[5] Philip Sidney, The Defence of Poesy, p.110.

replaced generosity. Yet, equally, Faustus' glaring deficiencies are manifested most clearly when contrasted with Sidney's _vates_: Faustus labors to achieve what for the genuine artist is divinely inspired. D.J. Palmer expresses this conjunction of magic illusions and dramatic imagination:

> As in _Tamburlaine_, Marlowe evidently conceives the stage as an area liberated from the limitations which nature imposes on the world around; the restraining conditions of probability here seem to be in abeyance, and Marlowe's stage affords scope to realise the gigantic fantasies of his heroes. In _Doctor Faustus_ the stage assumes the properties of a magic circle, within which dramatic spectacle is transformed into enchanted vision, and poetry is endowed with the power of conjuring spirits.[6]

Once again the overreaching of the magician is tied to our imaginative attempts to nullify the constraints upon us; once again we have a dramatic exploration of the alternatives to Aristotelian mimesis, marvelous illusions and shows whose magic exposes itself in the violation of temporal and spatial logic. Faustus' presentation and description of his own shows suggest that his magic produces no genuinely golden worlds: Faustus' shows, at once imitations and distortions of reality, never improve upon it, and remain self-serving and trivial.

Yet if the results are tawdry, the method is a serious exercise of imagination. Magic joins and severs distinct objects, separate places and times, asserts Faustus:

---

[6] D.J. Palmer, "Magic and Poetry in _Doctor Faustus_," revised and rpt. in _Marlowe_: Doctor Faustus: _A Casebook_, ed. John Jump (London: Macmillan, 1969), p. 188.

67

> Had I as many soules, as there be Starres,
> I'de giue them all for Mephostophilis.
> By him, I'le be great Emperour of the world,
> And make a bridge, through the mouing Aire,
> To passe the Ocean:  with a band of men
> I'le ioyne the Hils that bind the Affrick shore,
> And make that Country, continent to Spaine,
> And both contributary to my Crowne.
> The Emperour shall not liue, but by my leaue,
> Nor any Potentate of Germany.
> Now that I haue obtain'd what I desir'd
> I'le liue in speculation of this Art
> Till Mephostophilis returne againe. (I.iii.327-39)

Faustus would like to be thought "as cunning as Agrippa was" (I.i.139). Charles Masinton suggests that Faustus' reference to Agrippa follows so closely upon his mention of the legendary Greek poet Musaeus as to imply a connection between the arts of magic and poetry in Faustus' mind.[7] Whether or not this is true, the magic Faustus describes operates both as Agrippa's art of "joining and knitting ...together" things which are separate in Nature[8] and a poetic imagination which, according to Francis Bacon, "being not tied to the laws of matter, may at pleasure join that which nature has severed, and sever that which nature hath joined; and so make unlawful matches and divorces of

---

[7] Charles Masinton, Christopher Marlowe's Tragic Vision, p.120.

[8] Agrippa, The Philosophy of Natural Magic, pp. 38-39: the whole passage reads thus:  "Magic is a faculty of wonderful virtue, full of most high mysteries, containing ... the knowledge of whole Nature, and it doth instruct us concerning the differing and agreement of things amongst themselves, whence it produceth its wonderful effects, by uniting the virtues of things through the application of them one to the other, and to their inferior suitable subjects, joining and knitting them together thoroughly by the powers and virtues of the superior Bodies."

68

things."[9] Marlowe weights Faustus' magic by describing its method in terms consistent with that of less esoteric arts of the imagination.

For if Faustus does not actually bridge oceans or join Africa to Spain, he does display an astonishing ability to throw himself around the world: his magic justifies Marlowe's dramatic violation of the unities. The play opens with Faustus in his study, contemplating an art which he believes can resolve all ambiguities by including all possibilities. Magic brings, Faustus thinks, all corners and epochs of the world within the orbit of his mind:

> Shall I make spirits fetch me what I please?
> Resolue me of all ambiguities?
> Performe what desperate enterprise I will?
> I'le haue them flie to India for gold;
> Ransack the ocean for Orient Pearle,
> And search all corners of the new-found-world
> For pleasant fruites, and Princely delicates.
> I'le haue them read me strange Philosophy,
> And tell the secrets of all forraine Kings:
> I'le haue them wall all Germany with Brasse,
> And make swift Rhine, circle faire Wittenberge:
> I'le haue them fill the publicque Schooles with
> skill,
> Wherewith the Students shall be brauely clad.
> I'le leauy souldiers with the coyne they bring,
> And chase the Prince of Parma from our Land,
> And raigne sole King of all the Prouinces.
> (I.i.106-21)

We realize already that Faustus' desire to contain all that is outside himself can only be achieved at the expense of geographical sense and integrity.

---

[9] Francis Bacon, The Advancement of Learning (1605), in The Advancement of Learning and New Atlantis, ed. Thomas Case (London: Oxford Univ. Press, 1906.1974), p. 96.

69

The same pursuit of diminishing returns may be said to characterize both Marlowe's and Faustus' assaults on time, specifically on the restrictions time imposes on theater and life. Doctor Faustus spans twenty-four years instead of hours: Marlowe suggests simultaneously the law of writ and the liberty, highlighting his deviation from temporal unity but not crystallizing what is substituted in its place. The detail floats on the surface of the play, not firmly anchored to its structural depths. Marlowe's departure from temporal unity is but a limited relaxation of the normal restrictions on the dramatist: he inflates Faustus' time by a fixed proportion, furnishing the magician with only as many years as the dramatist was traditionally allowed hours. The violation of the dramatic convention is not an end in itself for Marlowe, but serves (as the dramatist's theatrical version of the devil's contract) precisely to indicate that Faustus' impression of temporal mercies received is illusory, and to deny the grand possibilities that Faustus envisages for the future. Yet that denial is only sketched, and we, like the hero, conveniently forget the terminal nature of this temporary freedom.

Faustus, revelling in his temporal extension, spends it heedlessly. He occupies his "foure and twenty yeares of liberty" (III.i.862) not just in flying round the globe and through the cosmos, but travelling through time, making nonsense of its usual restrictions. With his skill and

70

supernatural aides he conjures into the present time, and into appearance right now in front of him on the stage, such historically remote figures as Alexander the Great and Darius King of Persia. Faustus' effort to bring all time, like all space, into his own province does not of course succeed in making all times one and the same with the present. Where Marlowe deliberately breaks the unities in the play, Faustus tries for another kind of unity, hoping to fuse all the experience of men through the ages in his own twenty-four years, a bid to achieve an imaginative union with all that has been known and thought in the world. This leads only to the loss of personal independence, since Faustus can advance in knowledge and power only by conceding the advantage to a higher authority.

This Marlovian habit of yoking mutually destructive forces together informs the peculiarly double time and space of the entire play. D.J. Palmer brilliantly exposes the temporal and spatial paradoxes of Faustus' final agony:

> One cannot say which is the more "real," the illusion of a vast scene embracing heaven, earth and hell, or the illusion of a stage that has shrunk to cramping dimensions. But both are mutually dependent. Faustus is at bay, trapped in a corner, and yet his end is a universal drama ... a similar duality [exists] in the plane of time, each equally illusory. Faustus is no trapped by the clock, and by a bold theatrical device time passes with unerring swiftness: the minutes have diminished to seconds, just as the stage seems to have contracted, and closed in upon the doomed man. Yet we are aware too of timeless infinity, of the imminence of perpetual damnation.[10]

[10] D.J.Palmer,"Magic and Poetry," pp. 201-202.

71

The final deflation of the dimensions of stage and magician, which exactly counterbalances the initial inflation of time and space (into twenty-four years of unrestricted travel), is however foreshadowed in the early part of the play. Faustus' study has a double spatial connotation: it makes one little world an everywhere. It is the place that hides and isolates Faustus from his fellow scholars. But the place of seclusion and exclusiveness, suggests Cornelius, will bring all men to Faustus:

> The miracles that magick will performe,
> Will make thee vow to study nothing else.
> He that is grounded in Astrology,
> Inricht with tongues, well seene in Minerals,
> Hath all the Principles Magick doth require:
> Then doubt not Faustus but to be renowm'd,
> And more frequented for this mysterie,
> Then heeretofore the Delphian Oracle.(I.i.158-65)

The study of magic results paradoxically in both obscurity and fame, as its boundaries can both expand and contract: the potential blessings are from the beginning tied directly to evils. The physical space of Faustus' study takes on the proportions of hell, which

> hath no limits, nor is circumscrib'd,
> In one selfe place: but where we are is hell,
> And where hell is there must we ever be.(II.i.513)

Here lie the dangers of making one little room an everywhere: Faustus' study, like hell, is like the imagination, which can take us anywhere, but from which we can never escape.

The magician's unlimited freedom is thus itself an illusion. Faustus, perhaps unwittingly, suggests that all the places  and infinities of time he has seen in his travels are shows, implicitly illusions rather than realities:

> Thou know'st within the compass of eight daies,
> We view'd the face of heaven, of earth and hell.
> So high our Dragons soar'd into the aire,
> That looking downe the earthe appear'd to me,
> No bigger than my hand in quantity.
> There did we view the Kingdomes of the world,
> And what might please mine eye, I there beheld.
> Then in this shew let me an Actor be,
> That this proud Pope may Faustus comming
> see.(III.i.870-78)

But the Pope scenes, in which Faustus is an actor, are shows largely arranged by him, shows that are explicitly illusions, devised by magic. Faustus, like Marlowe, creates discontinuous dramatic episodes that are deliberate exercises in magic ingenuity, imaginative stretching of the mind. Faustus is caught, as I believe Marlowe is caught, in the confusion of his own making. As both an actor and a (surrogate) playwright, Faustus is both subject and controller of illusions. Faustus' improbable shows, magically bodying forth the creatures of a wanton imagination, are not finally proof against competition from

73

realities, because the magician's imagination takes him further than he can legitimately reach. Faustus' magic paradoxically divorces him from everything outside his imagination; initially the apparent manipulator of the magic circle within which devils may be commanded and "spirits ... inforc'd to rise" (I.iii.234-41), Faustus finds himself increasingly circumscribed within it. His sphere of action steadly shrinks under outside pressures. His final disintegration as an independent power is anticipated by a recurring imagery of disembodiment. The magician and his magic fall apart; the center cannot hold: Faustus' illusions of material realities, created out of air, display a tendency to break up, or dissolve into nothingness. The fragility of his magic shows signals the ephemerality of the products of all art, and the bottom drops out of the play: Marlowe's artistic self-consciousness, reflected in Faustus' exuberant dramaturgy, self-destructs. The following pages trace in Faustus' illusions the seeds of their own demise.

Faustus' control of illusion and magic is "learned" or transmitted by devilish spirits. These, like actors, are shape-changers, but unlike actors, engage in more than representation: they are impersonators as well. Valdes tells Faustus:

> So shall the spirits of every element,
> Be alwaies seruiceable to us three:
> Like Lyons shall they guard us when we please,
> Like Almaine Rutters with their horsemens staues,
> Or Lopland Giants trotting by our sides,

74

> Sometimes like women or unwedded Maides:
> Shadowing more beauty in their Airie browes,
> Then has the whilt breasts of the Queene of loue.
> (I.i.144-51)

The devil's spirits show Faustus how to conjure material shapes out of nothing. They arrange a dance of devils for Faustus in II.i which shows Faustus, as yet only the Devil's apprentice in sorcery, "what Magicke can perform" (471). Faustus takes on the privileges of the Devil's spirits. This, as the end of the play makes clear, gives him only the illusion of the deity he seeks ("Here tire my braines to get a Deity", I.i.89): though he becomes, through his contract with the Devil, "a spirit in forme and substance," this is only a cheap, false imitation of godly spirituality. Indeed theater in this play is associated as much with diabolic invention as with magic: if Marlowe sees himself in the magician, as is at least partly true from the beginning and I believe wholly true by the end of the play, then he is loading the dice against himself from the beginning, either in defiance or self-defence. Faustus acquires the devilish spirits' histrionic gifts, and is endowed by Lucifer with the power to "turne they selfe into what shape thou wilt" (II.ii.736-37). Theater for Faustus and the spirits is nothing more than self-indulgence of material and physical cravings. The woman-devil who materializes to serve Faustus' lust (II.i.536) sets a precedent for Faustus: if the constructions of other sympathetic magicians in the Renaissance realized desires with a degree of

75

dispassionateness, Faustus' illusions of material substance realize his concupiscent dreams or exploit those of somebody else.

The dangers inherent in such a practice are lost on Faustus: the idea that the deceptions of such magic augur against dependence on it never takes firm hold of his mind. In fact, seduced by Lucifer and Beelzebub, he soon loses sight of the distinction between the illusion and reality of bodily substance. The princes of hell, "come from hell in person to show thee some pastime," invite him to "sit downe and ... behold the seven deadly sinnes appeare to thee in their owne proper shapes and likenesse" (II.ii.669ff.). The physical form taken by the seven deadly sins is allegorical, only the outward and visible sign of what really counts, their inward nature. But the devils' speech suggests the opposite, and Faustus is gently led to concentrate on surfaces instead of depth, on appearances rather than real truth. Material substance in the play early on becomes a kind of debased currency, not a reliable token of true value, but a deceptive illusion camouflaging the opposite.

The constructions of Faustus' imagination and magic, the shows in which he plays and directs, are thus more properly delusions than illusions. In Act III he tells Mephostophilis to follow the cardinals to the Consistory and put them to sleep,

> And make them sleep so sound, that in their shapes,
> Thy selfe and I, may parly with this Pope.(924-25)

Raymond welcomes Faustus and Mephostophilis as "graue Fathers" (977), not seeing below the surface to the devilish spirits within. Later Faustus and Mephostophilis enter to the banquet "in their own shapes" (o.s.d.), and our vision is irresistibly directed to contemplation of what those shapes conceal. Marlowe repeatedly suggests a vacuity below the rich surfaces of things. Faustus requests Mephostophilis to make him magically invisible when confronting the Cardinals:

>              so charme me here,
> That I may walke inuisible to all,
> And do what ere I please, unseene of any. (1025-28)

Faustus has, as it were, traded in his disguise as Cardinal for the illusion of no form or material substance at all. The gift of invisibility carries a latent and dangerous irony in the Faustian world that substitutes shows and surfaces for realities and depth: Faustus may, we surmise here, do his disappearing act once too often, and be completely annihilated.

Yet Faustus the dramatist is fully aware of the distinction between illusion and substance, and knows that his shows are insubstantial. At the beginning of Act IV Martino announces that Faustus, "The wonder of the world for Magick Art" is coming to the emperor of Germany

>              to show great Carolus,
> The race of all his stout progenitors;
> And bring in presence of his Maiesty
> The royall shapes and warlike semblances
> Of Alexander and his beauteous Paramour.
>                 (IV.i.1190-97)

77

These are "What wonders by black spels may compast be" (1226), Martino advises us, without irony. Martino's contribution to the play's entanglement of artistic success with moral failure, of wonders with cheap tricks of necromancy, goes unchallenged at this point, but his confusion of semblance with real presence is immediately undone by Faustus when he introduces his show of Alexander. Here the A-text is indispensable, for it sharpens the distinction Faustus draws in both texts between material reality and the immaterial illusions of art. In the B-text Faustus explains the illusoriness of his show merely by indicating that since it is a magic spell, it requires silence if it is to succeed.[11]

> My lord, I must forewarne your Maiesty,
> That when my Spirits present the royal shapes
> Of Alexander and his Paramour,
> Your grace demand no questions of the king,
> but in dumb silence let them come and goe.
> (1281-85)

What the audience sees, and what the Emperor tries physically to embrace, "are but shadowes, not substantiall" (1305), cautions Faustus, in the B-text. There is a terrible irony in Faustus' failure here to connect the Emperor's embrace of shadows with his own. In the A-text Faustus both clarifies the immaterial nature of his shows and links it to his own limitations. Faustus admits "it

[11] See Marlowe, Doctor Faustus, ed. Roma Gill (London: Benn, 1965), IV.ii.44-48, for one of many notes on the connection between magic and silence.

78

is not in my abilitie to present before your eyes, the true substantiall bodies of those two deceased princes which long since are consumed to dust ... But such spirites as can lively resemble Alexander and his Paramour" (A-text,1081 ff.).[12] Faustus does not however connect this specific inadequacy in his power with the more general weakness of his magical and dramatic program: he habitually forgets the emptiness of his enterprise, in his enjoyment of the material wealth that enterprise appears to shower on him. Fundamentally deluded, he overlooks the danger that lies in becoming, himself, another insubstantial show.

For Faustus' early and brief transformation of himself and Mephostophilis into the unreal imitation of cardinals heralds his degeneration into the superficial show of a man, a shell that must inevitably break apart. Faustus becomes a hollow man, the shadow of his former self. The scenes involving Benvolio indicate not merely the fragility of Faustus' magic shows, but of the magician himself. Faustus' very person is subjected to the physical strains to which he subjects Benvolio, in retaliation for Benvolio's slights on the magician's dramatic power. Benvolio had sneered: "and thou bring Alexander and his Paramour before the Emperour, Il'e be Acteon, and turne myself to a Stagge" (1287-89). Faustus' revenge is therefore derivative: he copies Benvolio's idea, and translates his detractor, "In bold

[12] My only quotation of the A-text.

Acteons shape to turne a Stagge" (1344). The
magician-dramatist thus casts himself, as he promised
originally (1290), to "play Diana, and send you the hornes."
Faustus is thus the thing seen, the passive feminine
perpetually hunted, and on display. Of course Diana the
chaste is also mistress of the chase: goddesses, and
magicians, as we soon discover, are allowed an active role
as well. Faustus, in hot pursuit of Benvolio, becomes, in
Benvolio's words, "that damned Hell-hound" (1404) of the
type that Diana sent after Acteon-turned-stag. The magician
has, here, a double role, at once the hunter and the hunted,
able both to attract and chase his prey: but the strength
he draws from this initially strategic contradiction
dissipates as the scene progresses. The hell-hound pursuing
the stag suddenly becomes the target of the chase: Faustus
is ambushed by Benvolio and his friends in a grove.
Hell-hound and Acteon have apparently changed places. The
ambushers try to behead Faustus and divide his body:
Faustus is now the stag being torn to pieces. Benvolio even
plans to "naile huge forked hornes" on Faustus' head
(1431-32). The magician of course revives, and consigns his
pursuers to torment and dismemberment. Benvolio and his
fellow knights enter with horns and go to live in obscurity.
But Benvolio has held the stage long enough to suggest that
Faustus control of his show, and of his own part in that
show, is now at best intermittent.

80

These intimations of Faustus' imminent disintegration are repeated in the horse-courser scene. Again, the images of dismemberment and disembodiment transfer themselves from the subjects of Faustus' magic to the magician himself. Faustus sells a horse to the horse-courser for forty dollars, warning him not to ride it into the water. This natuarally prompts the horse-courser to do just that, and his horse disappears, dissolving as it were into the river, leaving nothing under the horse-courser "but a little straw" (1556). Roma Gill notes that running water was traditionally thought to dissolve a magic spell.[13] But the detail has a larger function than Gill's explanation implies. Faustus is obviously setting up the horse-courser for a fall: Faustus' magic thus actually exploits its own vulnerability to dissolution, and Faustus intends the illusory horse to dissolve. But what Faustus doubtless does not intend is the concomitant irony of the episode: he does to the horse-courser what will be done to him, depriving the horse-courser of his vehicle of transportation as he, the magician, will be deprived of his when his magic power finally dissolves and he is rendered impotent. As always, Marlowe turns the tables on the magician, confirms our growing sense of Faustus' personal vulnerability: the horse-courser now does to Faustus much what Faustus has done to his horse, pulling off Faustus' leg, trying to dismember

[13] Marlowe, Doctor Faustus, ed. Roma Gill, IV.v.12, note.

81

the vendor of the now disembodied horse. As in the Benvolio scenes, the magician's victim strikes back at the magician in a way that suggests the mutual reflection between disintrating magic shows or contrivances, and deteriorating magician.

The cumulative effect of these scenes is to indicate Faustus' assimilation to his own magic accomplishments, his self-destructing shows. As early as Act II the evil angel tells Faustus that if he repents, "devils will teare thee in peeces" (650); in fact as the play goes on to show, scene by scene, it is the exercise of black magic rather than repentance of it that ultimately tears Faustus apart. Faustus becomes as ephemeral as his unreal shows. The true signal of the magician's collapse lies not just in his diminished influence and substance, but in the way he takes on the color of his various endeavors. His unwilled imitation of his own creations negates the fundamental principle behind his magic and Marlowe's art, which is to reach beyond nature and transform it, not to imitate what already exists. The magician and artist should strive to out do themselves, to create something of greater value and permanence than nature affords us, at least according to contemporary theorists of both arts. Faustus' trivial exercise of magic power debases not only the art but, inevitably, his own soul. Acquisitiveness has replaced aspiration, which in turn is replaced by mere

82

destructiveness. Harry Levin notes the gap between the possibilities and achievements of Faustus' magic:

> We might have expected more for the price he is paying, after his terrible renunciation, than the jaunty hocus-pocus that produces grapes out of season for a pregnant duchess or defrauds a horse dealer and fobs him off with a leg-pulling practical joke ... we ought to feel some incongruity between the monologues and the gestures, between the seemingly unlimited possibilities envisioned by Faustus' speeches and their all too concretely vulgar realization in the stage business.[14]

Such "concretely vulgar realization" tends, furthermore, to be dissipated at the whim of the magician: Faustus' fatal egotism tempts him to prove his virtuosity again and again by capriciously undermining his own illusions, breaking up his own shows. Thus he spends his spirit in a waste of shame: the "seemingly unlimited possibilities" of magic as they appear in his monologues are from the beginning the baseles fabric of a fading vision. Faustus' "inchanted Castle in the Aire" (erected for the Vanholts, 1639-43) perhaps recalls Prospero's cloud-capped towers, but certainly stands as an image of those enchanted shows and insubstantial pageants that dissolve into thin air.

The crucial difference between Marlowe and Shakespeare here is the extent to which author identifies himself with the fallibility of the magician. Shakespeare's vision of art contains and thus supersedes Prospero's as Marlowe's

[14] Harry Levin, The Overreacher, pp. 120-21.

83

does not supersede Faustus'. Marlowe's greater pessimism about the power of art to work magic on our senses emerges in his choice of genre and in the irony surrounding his choice of magician. **Faustus is a translation of the name** Prospero,[15] but as Harry Levin notes: "That Faustus meant 'well-omened' in Latin was a paradox which did not pass unobserved."[16] The projected prosperities at the conclusion of The Tempest are consumed in the tragic end of Doctor Faustus. Ferdinand and Miranda assume Prospero's burden of improving their surroundings and fellow men; together they walk into a happy future, and together they embody the promise of new life in a brave new world. But the promises that we associate with magic, and that are embodied in Faustus' name and person, are savagely denied in the end of Marlowe's play. The discordant notes sounded in The Tempest by Prospero's personal inner conflicts do not seriously impinge on the concords of the ending; in contrast the internal contradictions of Marlowe's Faustus are major stumbling blocks in the way of magic transformation and the amendment of nature.

For Faustus' love of center stage defeats his function as a magician. Instead of reaching imaginatively beyond his own experience to benefit the collective experience of all men, Faustus' effort to contain all knowledge, worlds and

[15] Robert Egan, Drama within Drama (New York: Columbia Univ. Press, 1975), p. 97.

[16] Harry Levin, The Overreacher, p. 109.

84

times, an extremity of self-indulgence, paradoxically imposes the opposite extreme on Faustus, deprives him of a unified and coherent selfhood. Mephostophilis, calling Faustus to account in Act V, threatens the magician with personal fragmentation:

> Thou traytor Faustus, I arrest they soule,
> For disobedience to my soveraigne Lord,
> Revolt, or I'le in peece-meale tear thy flesh.
> (1847-49)

Faustus' aspirations reveal their worst perversity when he calls for the vision of Helen to make him immortal with a kiss (1874): he is reaching down, to hell, instead of up to better things, trying to over-reach the devil instead of reaching to Olympian heights. The false paradise afforded concupiscent lovers is here complicated and further debased by the fact of Helen's spirituality: copulation between body and spirit was one of the gravest of sins (1946). (Faustus' spirituality "in form and substance," vouchsafed him by the devil's contract, now seems either to have been forgotten or to have proved another illusion.)

Faustus' descent during the play from an exalted vision of magic's capabilities to a last desperate bid to outwit perdition, is a descent more apparent than real, however. In fact his early ambitions reflect his illusions about magic and about himself, and the superficial transformations

See, for example, W. W. Greg, "The Damnation of Faustus," rpt. in Marlowe: A Collection of Critical Essays, ed. Clifford Leech (Englewood Cliffs, N.J.: Prentice-Hall, 1964), pp. 105-106.

85

he effects in the middle acts betray his initial irresponsibility and delusions about the exercise and purpose of his magic. It is only at the end that Faustus comes to a firm realization of his error, but the error has of course been made at the beginning. His "descent" in Act V is more accurately a final and crushing disillusionment about his own career, as his exemption from time and its revenges simply runs out.

The conclusion of Doctor Faustus presents perhaps Marlowe's most damning comment on his own art. His magician, so patently a surrogate dramatist, and so obviously a dramatist straining beyond the confines of the commonplace and the ordinary, is finally consigned to hell. Nor is Faustus' defeat accomplished without a concerted expression of censure. Mephostophilis arrogantly condemns him: the magician's

> labouring braine,
> Begets a world of idle fantasies,
> To over-reach the Divell; but all in vaine, --
> His store of pleasures must be sauc'd with paine.
> (1908-11)

This is the end of magic and imagination in Marlowe: this is all the profit and delight that his "Studious Artizan" can expect. The magician's dominion, thought Faustus at the beginning, was limited only by his imagination, "Stretcheth as farre as doth the mind of man." This turns out to be a cruel allowance: it is the constraint of individual imagination for which Marlowe laments in Act V of his play.

And failure to reach successfully beyond the self, to achieve imaginative apotheosis, means not some neutral stasis, or a restoration of what one was before, but perpetual and conscious confinement in that constricted self, which is something worse. Faustus at the end actually craves the dismemberment and disembodiment to which his magic has apparently led him, because the breaking up of his personal imaginative vision turns out, against all expectation aroused by the imagery of the play, specifically to deny any such comforting disintegration:

> No end is limited to damned soules.
> Why wert thou not a creature wanting soule?
> Or why is this immortall that thou hast?
> O Pythagoras Metemsycosis; were that true,
> This soule should flee from me, and I be chang'd
> Into some brutish beast.
> All beasts are happy, for when they die,
> Their soules are soon dissolv'd in elements,
> But mine must live still to be plagu'd in hell.
> (2071-79)

Faustus cannot, in hell, transform himself into any lower state, any more brutish form than that which he has already achieved. Nor can he, like beasts, lose himself in death.

Up to this point all his degenerative transformations of people into the semblance of animals, and all the disintegrating shows, have cumulatively seemed to foreshadow Faustus' final deterioration, because he has consistently mirrored the shows and illusions his magic engenders. Marlowe's sudden explicit denial of such an end for Faustus does violence to the play's coherence, though there is, I

believe, some deliberacy behind the move. It is perhaps
his effort to prevent even a negative resolution of
Faustus' conflict: Marlowe seems bent on freezing the
internal contradictions of his magician in interminably
suspended animation. The magician, like the artist,
suggests Marlowe, is doomed to a perpetual vision of the
golden fruits of imagination and an infinite incapacity to
grasp them. Arguments for or against Faustus' final
repentance are, in the last analysis, a little beside the
point: whether or not Marlowe personally endorsed the view
that condemns Faustus, whether or not he saw art and magic
as inherently and unambiguously sinful (and it seems
inconceivable to me that he did), the damnation of Faustus
takes place anyway, and proves Marlowe's view of the
futility of such artistic imagination as he shares with his
magician. As the clock strikes midnight, Faustus
desperately wills his body to "turne to aire" and his soul
to "be chang'd into small water drops, and fall into the
Ocean ne're be found (2086-87). This imaginative effort to
drown the self by assimilation to all that is external to
it is uncharacteristic, and represents the last resort of
the despairing rather than a conversion to the true
selflessness that other playwrights suggest is required for
the success of magic and artistic effort. It fails.

Magic and imagination produce no golden worlds, in
Marlowe's judgment: no ideal is wrought by the imaginative
unrealism, the magical illusions and discontinuities of his

dramaturgy. Faustus' magic disruption of time and space, and his illusory shows, are a debased alternative to the rich tapestry Sidney attributed to poetic representations of nature. What Marlowe offers in Doctor Faustus as a reflection on himself is a Faustian imagination constrained by egocentricity, fundamentally diseased,[18] and yet of a tragic grandeur and pathos. Marlowe's irony includes himself, and his own internal contradictions occasionally impinge like those of Faustus on the product of his imagination, the play itself. But it is a tragic irony: the last scenes play out not a triumphant or a deprecating apology for poetry, but the bitterness of its death-struggle. Marlowe does not allow his alter-ego to "go gentle into that good night":[19] Faustus' rebellion against the terms of his contract, however futile, reflects Marlowe's own rage against the dying of the light. The artist ends in hell, where there is no respite from his

[18] L. C. Knights, "The Orthodoxy of Faustus," in Twentieth Century Interpretations of Doctor Faustus, ed. Willard Farnham (Englewood Cliffs, N.J.: Prentice-Hall, 1969), p. 99, sees this as "a crucial gap in the play's imaginative structure. For where, we may ask, are the contrasting positives against which Faustus' misdirection of his energies could be measured?" The problem is obviated if we dispense with the assumption of rigid orthodoxy (without substituting a romantic belief in Marlowe's heterodoxy): the ironist is not obliged to present contrasting positives.

[19] Quoting here and at the end of the sentence from Dylan Thomas' "Do Not Go Gentle Into That Good Night" in The Poems of Dylan Thomas, ed. David Jones (New York: New Directions, 1971), pp. 207-208.

89

agonizing limitations, no release from the forces that have always and will always tear him in opposite directions.

Drama for Marlowe consists in perceived and unresolvable contradiction, in the tension created and sustained by unsatisfied desire, which in Doctor Faustus is the desire that spurs magic and imagination. He was unable or unwilling to dissipate this tension in the ending. Lawrence Danson quotes Richard Hooker in support of the thesis that Faustus is doomed because his desire is evil in itself:

> Now that which man doth desire with reference to a further end, the same he desireth in such measure as is unto that end convenient; but what he coveteth as good in itself, toward that his desire is ever infinite. So that unless the last good of all, which is desired altogether for itself, be also infinite, we do evil in making it our end.... Nothing may be infinitely desired but that good which is indeed infinite.... No good is infinite but only God.[20]

But if Marlowe ever, even occasionally, condemned his own imagination as a spiritual frailty, it seems unlikely to me that he consistently censured the strong desires that animate all his tragic heroes. He seems rather to have mourned their eternal, inevitable and tragic unfulfillment: whatever Marlowe's real moral position (if in fact he had determined it), his explicit stance is mordantly

[20] Richard Hooker, Of the Laws of Ecclesiastical Polity [1953], Book 1, Chap. 11 (London: 1907, rpt. 1963), 1:202-203, cited in L. Danson, "Christopher Marlowe: The Questioner," ELR (Winter 1982), p. 23.

90

and reflexively ironic. The whole movement of the play
dynamically enacts and draws us onto the horns of Faustus'
dilemma.

J. B. Steane characterizes Doctor Faustus as a
"to-and-fro of extremes,"

> a play of violent contrasts within a rigorous
> structural unity. Hilarity and agony, seriousness
> and irresponsibility: even on the most cautious
> theories of authorship, Marlowe is responsible at
> times for all these extremes. This artistic
> instability matches the instability of the hero.
> The extremes of optimism and depression,
> enthusiasm and hatred, commitment to Hell and
> aspiration to Heaven, pride and shame: these are
> the swings of the pendulum in Faustus' world, and
> they are reflected by the sickening to-and-fro
> motion of the verse--an ambivalence first felt in
> the Prologue's "forme of Faustus' fortunes good or
> bad."[21]

Marlowe's portrait of an artist-magician pitched restlessly
between the antithetical extremes of infinite possibility
and limitation gives way, in Shakespeare, to a synthesis of
compromise and, increasingly, hope: Shakespeare visualizes
the release of the tension created by unsatisfied desire
either in tragic experience more completely cathartic than
Marlowe's (because Shakespeare leads us more clearly
through his own identification with and separation from the
hero), or, in his two plays of magic, through the
resolution of comedy. A Midsummer Night's Dream begins,
and The Tempest completes, the emancipation of magic and
imagination from Marlovian constraints.

[21] J. B. Steane, Marlowe, pp. 164-65.

## Chapter IV

### Anticipating the promised end: magical discontinuity in _A Midsummer Night's Dream_

There is possibly no more decisive route to an audience's trust than an overt assault on its confidence: the dramatist who in addition lets us connive at our own discomfiture usually commands our highest respect. Shakespeare, by a dazzling, simultaneous execution of such strategies, sometimes actually thwarts our expectations of comic or tragic endings precisely in the honoring of conventional guarantees. Before _King Lear_ can end, for example, Cordelia must be hanged and her father must die with her body in his arms: we know what is coming, and we sense it even if, miraculously, we are new to the story. Yet when Kent asks soberly if this is indeed "the promis'd end" (V.iii.262),[1] we recognize in a flash that we share his incredulity: the fulfilment of this generic promise seems now a betrayal.[2] Like Kent, identifying with and revolting against the mortification of Lear, we would if possible deny

---

[1] Shakespeare, _King Lear_, ed. Kenneth Muir, (London: Methuen, 1959).

[2] Of the many expressed doubts about the fitness of this ending, the most famous is undoubtedly Samuel Johnson's note, in _Johnson on Shakespeare_, ed. Arthur Sherbo, Vol VIII of _The Yale Edition of the Works of Samuel Johnson_ (New Haven: Yale Univ. Press, 1968), pp. 703-704.

92

this tragedy its legitimate and long-expected conclusion. Shakespeare's extraordinary achievement in _Lear_ is to force our consent to something we thought we had already accepted. The play systematically discloses the anomaly of tragic endings that can be foreseen from the beginning but seen feelingly only at the end. And perhaps not accepted even then: the worst is not so long as we can say this is the worst.

There is a comparable anomaly in certain of Shakespeare's comic endings. Helen Gardner argues, conventionally, that "comedy contrives an end which is not implicit in its beginning,"[3] as is tragedy's: some comic twist arrests and reverses an otherwise potentially tragic movement,[4] and the ending is not inevitable but evitable, surprising. But any audience worth its salt knows perfectly well that it is watching a comedy, and thus actually expects such a "surprise" ending. The promise inherent in comic structure therefore competes directly with the promise of genre itself; the comic playwright is obliged to surprise us against the odds.

[3] Helen Gardner, "As You Like It," in _More Talking Of Shakespeare_, ed. J. Garrett (Freeport: Books for Libraries Press, 1970), p. 21.

[4] Gardner, "As You Like It," pp. 21-23; see also the standard argument in Northrop Frye, "The Argument of Comedy," _English Institute Essays_, 1948 (1949), rpt. in _Shakespeare: Modern Essays in Criticism_, ed. L. F. Dean (New York: Oxford, 1957), p. 84.

93

Shakespeare meets the challenge variously. He may mute the joy of comic endings, thus denying complete fulfilment of generic expectation, as in Twelfth Night. Or he may take the action so close to tragedy before allowing a comic ending that the element of surprise is strengthened: this, arguably, is the strategy in the "dark" comedies. Or finally, as in the so-called "happy" comedies,[5] he experiments with a paradox, and anticipates that fundamental principle of comic endings, surprise itself. A Midsummer Night's Dream defies audience's auguries about its ending because the element of surprise pervades the play. When comic twists and sudden reversals of progress occur throughout the action, and not just at the end, our ability and indeed our inclination to predict outcomes are substantially weakened. The promised end recedes from our field of vision, as the surprise-principle of ending becomes immanent rather than imminent (to borrow from Kermode), during the play.[6]

This chapter undertakes first to describe the surprises and twists in the play's progress, and then to define the precise role of fairy magic in creating those upsets. Few critics miss the obvious identification of artist and

[5] In J. Dover Wilson, Shakespeare's Happy Comedies (London: Faber, 1962).

[6] Frank Kermode, The Sense of an Ending: Studies in the Theory of Fiction (New York: Oxford Univ. Press, 1967), p.30.

94

magician, wherever magicians appear.[7] Both create temporal and spatial illusions. Close reading of A Midsummer Night's Dream suggests however that simple identification of the two does not do justice to Shakespeare's more complex achievement. I examine the extent to which the fairy magicians are Shakespeare's agents of change, the medium through which he figures and disfigures temporal and spatial "reality." But extents necessarily have limits. The demonstrable inadequacy of Oberon's power in turn demonstrate something else: a distance between Shakespeare and the magicians that is occasionally as divisive as that between Shakespeare and Theseus. Shakespeare explores the limits of his analogy between magic and art as enthusiastically as he establishes the analogy's truth. I therefore follow my discussion of the magicians' influence on temporal and spatial progress with an attempt to locate the limits of their power, the points at which time and space begin to control them; their magic power has virtually dissolved by the ending.

[7] On art and magic in A Midsummer Night's Dream see e.g. J. Dennis Huston, Shakespeare's Comedies of Play (New York: Columbia Univ. Press, 1981), who notes, p. 112, the manipulation of space and time common to artists and magicians, though sensibly distinguishing (p. 113) Oberon's and Shakespeare's powers; see also Sidney Homan, When the Theater Turns to Itself (Lewisburg: Bucknell Univ. Press, 1981), pp. 80, 93; W.O. Scott, The God of Arts (Lawrence: Univ. of Kansas Publications, 1977), p.110.

95

A Midsummer Night's Dream is in its own way as attentive as Lear to the condition of ending. Critics have placed the "real" ending of the play as early as IV.i.;[8] others observe the curious series of "false endings" in Act V.[9] As the artisan players, Theseus, Oberon, and finally Puck each depart the stage, each individually announces the closure of action. Shakespeare contrives to suggest that none of them can put a period to the performance, and that endings can only be rehearsed. Act V enacts a sequence of false endings, the inverse of "false starts" that are the more usual error of performers unequal to their task. Yet while the action seems to proceed indefinitely into the future beyond the play, the tendency to forced closure seems to stretch at least as far back as Act I, Scene i. Quince may not have a very firm grip on "the true beginning of our end," or even on the multiple meanings of the word "end" itself, but the alert reader or playgoer will remember that the very first speeches of the play anticipate, and with considerable impatience, the end of action.

[8] R. W. Dent, "Imagination in A Midsummer Night's Dream," Shakespeare Quarterly 15.2 (1964), 115, thus can argue against a tendency in criticism to regard the play "as essentially complete in four acts, but with a fifth act somehow vaguely appropriate in mood and content to serve as a conclusion."

[9] Especially James E. Hirsch, The Structure of Shakespearean Scenes (New Haven: Yale Univ. Press, 1981),pp. 183-86; see also Albert Cook, Shakespeare's Enactment: The Dynamics of Renaissance Theatre (Chicago: Swallow Press, 1976), p. 183; Jorg Hasler, Shakespeare's Theatrical Notation: The Comedies (Bern: Franck, 1974), pp. 153-58 also links beginning and end.

Indeed the first scene actually defines what ending entails in A Midsummer Night's Dream. C. L. Barber draws attention to the imagery of dissolving and disembodiment that prevails in the opening exchanges: to end is not merely to cease being; it is to become physically insubstantial. "Hippolyta says that the four days until the wedding will 'quickly steep themselves in night' and the nights 'quickly dream away the time' (I.i.6-7) -- night will dissolve day in dream." Barber connects this with the imagery of imprints in wax that describes Hermia's relationship to her father: she is a "form in wax" and Egeus may "leave the figure, or disfigure it" (I.i.49-51).[10] Barber attributes such images to the exigencies of metamorphosis; they are also, however, significant images of temporal progress in the play. Metamorphosis after all, as an instant change of state, means a sudden end and new beginning; metamorphosis is itself a visualization of temporal discontinuity.

Transition in A Midsummer Night's Dream is intimately related to dissolution of scene and persons, and dissolving actors, visions, and pageants faded, are inevitably suggestive of ending. Things lose their customary shape in the forest: the forms connot hold. The features of the lovers are not merely similar; they are similarly unfixed and, increasingly, inchoate. As Demetrius and Lysander

[10] C. L. Barber, Shakespeare's Festive Comedy (Princeton: Princeton Univ. Press, 1959), p.133.

exchange personalities back and forth, visible and physical evidence loses its stability and integrity. Some critics note astutely that Puck's voice in the forest eventually replaces each lover's identity (briefly);[11] when we speak of the disembodiment of Demetrius and Lysander we are not being purely figurative.[12] Shakespeare himself, exercising both Egeus' options, chooses sometimes "to leave the figure" in place, and sometimes "to disfigure" his own creation, to erase his work. Theseus may define the poet as one who turns to shapes the forms of things unknown; his creator simultaneously allows that definition and, brilliantly, undefines it: local habitations and names can just as easily turn to airy nothing. The play trains us to feel that what we see may at any moment abruptly withdraw from view": slowly we learn that we cannot depend on a logical connection of one moment with the next. The Dream constructs itself upon non sequiturs, and the familiar features of time itself thus seem to blur before our eyes.

[11] E.g. Alexander Leggatt, Shakespeare's Comedy of Love (London: Methuen, 1974), p. 98.

[12] Marjorie B. Garber, Dream in Shakespeare: From Metaphor to Metamorphosis (New Haven: Yale Univ. Press, 1974), p. 77, defines the exact antithesis to my argument; she finds continuity in the play through its "fundamental structural principle ... that the creatures of the dream world enact literally what is undergone figuratively or metaphorically by the citizens of the court. The result is a kind of visual punning with the metaphors physically present on the stage." For a similar but briefer discussion see Jackson Cope, The Theater and the Dream: From Metaphor to Form in Renaissance Drama (Baltimore: Johns Hopkins Univ. Press, 1973), p. 224.

98

It is of course the passage of time itself that, in Hippolyta's opening suggestion, dissolves.  In practice, the play's repeated dissolutions and "endings" do not, as she hopes, close the gap between scene one and the wedding so much as they disclose magical discontinuities in the duration that must elapse between the play's opening and ending.

A review of the play as a discontinuous movement in time is needed to balance the critically current opposite view. The indisputably integrative atmosphere of the play's ending naturally prompts discussions of organic unity, and thus of origins and causes that demonstrate the continuity of dramatic development, the interdependence of beginning, middle, and end, and the interpenetration of the play's two worlds.[13] My focus on endings instead of beginnings reflects a conviction that the discontinuities of temporal structure are, equally, integral to the play's effectiveness. Alexander Leggatt is surely right in finding that the fragility of the play's final harmonies leaves as lasting and captivating an impression on audiences as the concord

---

[13] See e.g. David P. Young, Something of Great Constancy: The Art of "A Midsummer Night's Dream" (New Haven: Yale Univ. Press, 1966); of the many since Frye's "The Argument of Comedy" who define structural continuity in Shakespearean comedy through a perceived interpenetration of its two worlds see e.g. S. H. Hawkins, "The Two Worlds of Shakespearean Comedy," Shakespeare Studies, III (1967), 62-80; and more generally H. Berger, Jr., "The Renaissance Imagination: Second World and Green World," Centennial Review, 9 (Winter 1965), 36-78.

itself.[14] The sustained balance of the play's rich varieties is the more dramatic as it is a delicate balance.

A Midsummer Night's Dream's greatest vulnerability may be its popularity. Our familiarity with the play may dull our sensitivities to Shakespeare's acrobatics, his virtuoso juggling with the dramatic materials. Perhaps the only true constant in the Dream is that everything familiar must be put in jeopardy. No scene or character is static or fixed (though the degree of change may be slight),[15] and action is relentlessly restless. Getting from one place and time to another is difficult for the protagonists and inexplicable from the perspective of witnesses; moments do not follow one another in time-honored fashion and physical space does not obey the rules with which we are familiar. Puck can compass the globe in only forty minutes, since for him, distance and time are magically negotiable. Yet we find ourselves taking such feats for granted: if confusions and wonders are of magical origin, then they are a given of this kind of story (so the reasoning goes) and not to be belabored.[16] Dreams, we often add, are hardly susceptible to logical analysis.

[14] Leggatt, Shakespeare's Comedy of Love, pp. 111-15.

[15] Leah Scragg, "Shakespeare, Lyly and Ovid: The Influence of 'Gallathea' on 'A Midsummmer Night's Dream'," Shakespeare Survey, 30 (1977), p. 131, borrowing a line from Gallathea, describes both plays as "'constant in nothing but inconstancy'."

[16] See e.g. John Arthos, Shakespeare's Use of Dream and Vision (London: Bowes, 1977), p. 87.

So Shakespeare apparently wants us to think. But there is more to it than this. The dramatis personae bring considerable varieties of intelligence and intuitiveness to bear on their experiences in the forest: dare we settle for the dismissiveness of the least perceptive? The play is a test, and a kind of double bluff: the magical dream that overtly pretends to discourage logical analysis actually yields more of its force to those attentive to its oddity.

It is worth keeping our wits about us, and nowhere is this more salutary than at the moment when Theseus enters the forest at IV.i.102. Nowhere is transition more dramatically disjunct. Oberon and Titania have just left the scene; by the next line of poetry Athenians have replaced fairies as official guardians and arbiters of the action. One set of rulers appears to cede instantly to another; the magic wood undergoes instantaneous domestication into an Athenian suburb. The change is abrupt, total, significant: night, with all that night implies, is at last apparently dissolved in day.

The casualness of the transition is easily misread: it is tempting to see the flight of Titania and Oberon as cue for the entry of Theseus and his train, and indeed for the actors it is. But the scene's power depends on there being no exchange of signals between the two groups. It is the sublime disregard of each set of actors for the other that gives this moment of transition its dreamlike character and

101

its force; each group's innocence of the other's presence conveys the disjunction between their worlds, between night and day. It is daybreak. Theseus enters the forest with no thought of Oberon, and with no firmer purpose than to occupy the time that must elapse before the wedding night. He resumes at least nominal control of the action in complete ignorance of those magic forces, recently dislodged, whose very existence challenges his authority. But even more impressive is Oberon's failure to see Theseus, his erstwhile rival in love, and his competitor in rule, approaching with the dawn. For all his supernatural powers, Oberon is no more aware than Theseus of their proximity, and moves serenely off stage.

Shakespeare contrives a clear point of demarcation between what precedes and what follows this moment. The authorities of magic night and prosaic day meet and yet do not meet: two world converge in a common space at the same time, but do not touch. Their unwilled near-collision at IV.i.101-102 is Shakespeare's most dramatic articulation of the play's structural cesuras. Others may be mentioned more briefly. The replacement of Athens with forest in our field of vision is just as abrupt, and involves just as many non sequiturs as the point of return in Act IV, though there is less visual presentation of two colliding worlds. Though the fairies seem more aware than the courtiers, at least in the early stages of the play, that the two worlds partly

102

interpenetrate, the fairies do not initiate the entry of the lovers into the forest: their subsequent influence on the lovers reflects ultimately as much an agility in responding to events as a talent for engineering them.

The lovers, of course, are far worse engineers; what they hope for when they enter the forest bears no relation to what actually happens to them there. Even the most penetrating psychological explanation of the lovers' dreams cannot fully sustain an argument for complete continuity between the situation in Athens in Act I and the developments in the forest in Act II, if only because attaching psychological data to these lovers is, I would argue, a precarious operation.[17] There is, of course, a continuity of sorts; the cyclical movement from Athens to forest to Athens may suggest to the imaginative an infinitely repeatable process. But what is repeated is change; the worlds of the play each attract and repel, in turn, the travelling cast of characters. Both Athens and the forest share a tendency to form, disintegrate and

---

[17] Larry S. Champion, The Evolution of Shakespeare's Comedy (Cambridge: Harvard Univ. Press, 1970), pp. 47-49, goes further than I would, denying the characters any personality at all; on recent developments in psychoanalytic perspectives on A Midsummer Night's Dream see e.g. Norman Holland, "Hermia's Dream," The Annual of Psychoanalysis, 7 (1979), rpt. in Representing Shakespeare: New Psychoanalytic Essays, ed. Murray Schwartz and Coppelia Kahn (Baltimore: Johns Hopkins Univ. Press, 1980), pp. 1-20: Holland records, interestingly, his dissatisfaction with the transactive approach as explanation of the play's ending, and finds a discontinuity between the infidelities of the middle section and subsequent reconciliations.

reform, during the course of action, and progress is thereby continuously discontinuous.

The influence of the fairies on time and space is not of course restricted to the middle point of the cycle, the forest scenes: it is however at its greatest there, and there too, oddly, most fallible. Titania's early discussion with Oberon suggests this double truth:

> And never, since the middle summer's spring,
> Met we on hill, in dale, forest or mead,
> By paved fountain, or by rushy brook,
> Or in the beached margent of the sea,
> To dance our ringlets to the whistling wind,
> But with thy brawls thou hast disturbed our sport.
> Therefore the winds, piping to us in vain,
> As in revenge have suck'd up from the sea
> Contagious fogs; which, falling in the land,
> Hath every pelting river made so proud
> That they have overborne their continents.
> The ox hath therefore stretch'd his yoke in vain,
> The ploughman lost his sweat, and the green corn
> Hath rotted ere his youth attain'd a beard;
> The fold stands empty in the drowned field,
> And crows are fatted with the murrion flock;
> Therefore the moon, the governess of floods,
> Pale in her anger, washes all the air,
> That rheumatic diseases do abound.
> And thorough this distemperature we see
> The seasons alter: hoary-headed frosts
> Fall in the fresh lap of the crimson rose;
> And on old Hiems' thin and icy crown,
> An odorous chaplet of sweet summer buds
> Is, as in mockery, set; the spring, the summer,
> The childing autumn, angry winter, change
> Their wonted liveries; and the mazed world,
> By their increase, now knows not which is which.
> And this same progeny of evils comes
> From our debate, from our dissension;
> We are their parents and original. (II.i.82-117)

The fairies have power to influence space and time, to make everything in nature change its natural place, to disrupt

104

the regular seasonal cycles (which, as Marjorie Garber notes, means disturbing the normal agents of transformation).[18] But their power is not fully willed, and is thus not full power. Unable to control their own relationship, Oberon and Titania do not fully dictate the results of their quarrel, do not influence time and space exclusively at will.

Do the fairies do any better when consciously wielding their power? The dimensions of the wood are curiously fluid, its inhabitants considerably various in the matter of magnitude. As R.W. Dent notes, the disparity in size between the large Bottom and tiny Titania does not impede their love,[19] though it is a relief to learn that Bottom does not have to subsist for long without suitably man-size pecks of provender and bottles of hay: a diminished Bottom would be a dreadful thing.

But, more importantly, the forest has a confusing geography defying orientation; there are neither maps nor assurances that maps would help. The lovers, relying on memory and instinct to negotiate its terrain, immediately lose their way. Demetrius, in an apparent effort to declare complete mastery of the immediate environment, nastily warns Helena against trusting her virginity to "the opportunity of night and the ill counsel of a desert place" (II.i.217-19),

[18] Garber, Dream in Shakespeare, p. 75.

[19] R.W.Dent, "Imagination in A Midsummer Night's Dream," p. 126.

105

that is, he might almost say, to him. But projecting his own sense of oppression onto Helena does not help him find Lysander and Hermia. They, in turn, are similarly confounded by the strange interior of the forest: "I have forgot our way" (II.ii.35), Lysander ruefully tells Hermia.

Thus far the fairies' responsibility for the geographical confusions of the forest is unclear. But the progressive inhibition of direction-finding results directly from magic forces. Puck confuses the artisans by changing shape and pursuing them in circles: "I'll follow you: I'll lead you about a round!" (III.i.101). In this looking-glass landscape, all is inverted, and opposites equate. Following and leading are for all intents and purposes the same thing, and flight is construed in the forest as pursuit, or at least, aggression. So at least Bottom interprets his friends' departure: "Why do they run away? This is a knavery of them to make me afear'd" (107). He vows not to "stir from this place," in spite of the pressure he feels they are exerting on him to do so.

Puck repeats the technique with the lovers in III.ii.400ff. Following now Lysnader, now Demetrius, imitating the voice of each, he foils all their attempts to fix one anothers' bearings. Demetrius pants: "Thou runn'st before me, shifting every place" (422), and Lysander complains:

> He goes before me, and still dares me on:
> When I come where he calls, then he is gone.
> The villain is much lighter-heel'd than I;

  106

        I followed fast; but faster he did fly,
        That fallen am I in dark uneven way,
        And here will rest me. (413-18)

This is, dream-like, running fast and getting nowhere.
Hermia, like her lover, "can no further crawl, no further
go"; her "legs can keep no pace with (her) desires"
(444-45). The distance and the time seem interminable, as
Helena confirms: "O weary night, O long and tedious night,/
Abate thy hours!" (431-32).

    History is just as hard to establish as geography in the
forest. The precise chronology of events is notoriously
elusive.[20] It is night, fairy time (V.i.350), and a night,
moreover, of especial, magically reinforced blackness, which
compounds the difficulties in the way of temporal and
spatial orientation. The lovers discover a peculiar
inability to recount "the story of the night" (V.i.23).
This is not just a product of Oberon's last spell; the
fairies have so interfered with causes and effects in the
wood, and have so disrupted the sequence of events, that
memory has in any case very little clear data at the
disposal of any projected story-telling. Continuous,
sensible narrative depends primarily on logical sequence in
the thing to be narrated;[21] Bottom's efforts to express his

---

    [20] Anne Paolucci, "The Lost Days in A Midsummer Night's
Dream," Shakespeare Quarterly, 28.3 (1977), 317-26,
discusses the problem of chronology and tries to rescue
Shakespeare from charges of error in the play's time
structure.

    [21] Bottom's art is mimetic; it is noteworthy that the
ballad he plans to commission would be a written one that he

107

experience are foiled not just by his faulty memory, but by the inconsequentiality of the experience itself.

As soon as he wakes, he calls for his friends, as if forgetting their flight, and as if his "sleep" has lasted no time at all.[22] Yet, for all his forgetfulness, he knows he has had a "most rare vision" (IV.i.203), that much has occurred in the interval between the truncated rehearsal and his awakening. But it is a vision that cannot easily be told: again and again Bottom emphasizes his primary difficulty, which is the _telling_. He confidently proposes that Quince should write a ballad of his dream, though aware that it is "past the wit of man to say what dream it was" or what it comprised. His comic insistency on this point draws a sharp picture of the precise way magic has disturbed time; Bottom wants a narrative of something inaccessible to narration, something lacking either logic or continuity.

It is impossible, in other words, to "discourse wonders" (IV.11.28), to relate them in the continuous form Bottom pretends to promise his comrades -- were there time. As the lovers shortly discover, story-form is ill-suited to a magical sequence of events.[23] Fairies like Puck may prefer

could sing, and conforms to the type identified by R. Scholes and R. Kellogg, _The Nature of Narrative_ (New York: Oxford Univ. Press, 1966), p. 30, as a "pseudo-oral narrative" which is in fact a "fixed literary text."

[22] Given Bottom's probable ignorance of dreams' brevity, it is odd that he expects his friends to be within call, still, when he awakes.

[23] There seems insufficient evidence for the assertion

108

things "That befall prepost'rously" (III.ii.120-21), but mortal historians have other requirements. The essence of the fairies' magic, the love potion, is the alteration of ordinary predictable sequence: the juice of the "love-in-idleness"flower,

> on sleeping eyelids laid,
> Will make or man or woman madly dote
> Upon the next live creature that it sees.
> (II.i.170-72)

That is, the potion effects an instant, artificial sympathy between two formerly unconnected people, creating and mocking the arbitrary and facile qualities (as Shakespeare appears to conceive them) of love at first sight. The "next live creature" that the waking victim sees replaces all former loves, wipes out the past, and creates new lines of force between individuals, new couples, new configurations in the dance through the forest. This connection between love and magic is of the type described by Henry Cornelius Agrippa: "women, by certain strong dreams, and suggestions, brought in by certain magical arts, do often bind themselves into a strong affection for any one".[24] Shakespeare's lovers themselves speak of this "love" as a physical magnetic force: "What love could press Lysander from my side?"

of Harold Brooks, the Arden editor (at IV.ii.28-32), that the story the lovers eventually tell (off-stage between Acts IV and V) shows "an awareness of fairy participation they never possessed at the time."

[24] Henry Cornelius Agrippa, The Philosophy of Natural Magic, p. 203.

109

queries Hermia (III.ii.185), and her erstwhile fiance responds: "Lysander's love, that would not let him bide." This magically synthesized love "presses" him from her. Disturbing and redirecting the sequence of events and the pairing of their victims, the fairies indicate a formidable (though not inexhaustible) mastery of time and space in the forest, working always against reasonable and realistic expectation.

Indeed the comedy arises partly from the discrepancy between what the victim believes about his "vision," his new love, on awaking, and what witnesses see and know to be true and real. Oberon says, over the recumbent form of his queen: "What thou seest when thou dost wake,/ Do it for thy true love take" (II.ii.26-27); the "taking," the "believing" is the primary target of his magic, which engineers mistaking. Titania believes what we know is illusion: that Bottom plus ass-head is her one and only true love. The picture she makes of Bottom as lover, lying beside her in flowers, is one she is able, under magic influence, to find completely natural, though for the unenchanted it lacks all verisimilitude. We are of course implicated in her folly insofar as we must admit that what we find neither likely nor realistic is, manifestly, really happening before our eyes.

In just this way do the lovers' notions of the natural and the true change under magic influence. Lysander, waking

110

to a vision of Helena, expresses a willingness to "run
though fire" for her (II.ii.102). There is a superb irony
in his ardor:

> Transparent Helena! Nature shows art,
> That through thy bosom makes me see thy heart.
> (103-4)

Nature shows art indeed, art of a magic color. His vision
of Helena bears little relation to ours, and his, comically,
reduces what substantiality she has.[25]

The reaction of unaffected bystanders confirms the basis
of the fairies' strategies: what their magic fundamentally
does is to interfere with the canons of "reality." The
fairies tamper with the fundamental laws of evidence by
which we determine what really is. Hermia, faced with (or
rather without) her aberrant Lysander, voices bewilderment:

> I am as fair now as I was erewhile.
> Since night you lov'd me; yet since night you left
> me.
> (III.ii.274-75)

Mystified by the change, she can find nothing to account for
it; the fairies have exploited her reliance on the rational
assimilation of evidence (and of course thus have shown its
inadequacy). The inability of each lover to believe the
most vehement protests of all the others suggests their
collective vulnerability to pre-conceived notions of what

---

[25] The Arden ed. notes at II.ii.103, from Stanley
Wells's edition, that Lysander equates the art by which
Helena is rendered transparent with the art of magicians:
Lysander speaks more truly and foolishly than he knows.

constitutes reality. They are the more vulnerable as their reason itself is distinctly finite-- but that is another story. So in III.ii. Lysander and Helena cannot credit Demetrius' profession of love for Helena; Helena does not believe the protestations of love by either man, and Hermia cannot believe she is now quite unloved:

> I'll believe as soon
> This whole earth may be bor'd, and that the moon
> May through the centre creep, and so displease
> Her brother's noon-tide with the antipodes.
> (III.ii.52-55)

It is ironic that Hermia seizes on such spatial and temporal impossibility as an example of what she considers unbelievable, for the truth is no stranger than her fiction.[26] Shakespeare obligingly completes the symmetry of the lovers' collective predicament: Helena cannot believe Hermia does not believe neither man loves her. Shakespeare thus makes victims both of believers _and_ skeptics, here, and throughout the play.

Shakespeare's reconcilitation of mimetic and anti-mimetic or poetic impulses is at once like and yet a variation upon Sidney's. Richard Henze finds Shakespeare's answer to Sidney not of course in "Theseus' skeptical Platonism"[27] but

---

[26] Anne Paolucci, "The Lost Days," p. 324, argues, not quite convincingly, that Hermia's words here describe the actual temporal facts.

[27] Richard Henze, "A _Midsummer_ _Night's_ _Dream_: Analogous Image," _Shakespeare_ _Studies_, 7 (1974), 117, with succeeding reference in my text; Sidney, _The_ _Defence_ _of_ _Poesy_, pp. 108-10.

in a less idealizing, less moral art that stresses "credible verisimilitude and the analogous image" (p. 115). The situation is more complex that Henze allows, however. Shakespeare's wilful violation of the spatial and temporal unities upon which Sidney insisted hardly justifies a view of Shakespeare as hard-nosed "realist." Shakespeare's disregard for the rules is deliberate, and provides, as we shall see, a sophisticated and witty answer to such challenges as Sidney's censure of dramatists who represent the stage first as a garden, and then as something quite else: "By and by we hear news of shipwreck in the same place, then we are to blame if we accept it not for a rock" (p. 148). My chapter on _The Tempest_ goes more deeply into the relationship of Shakespeare's and Sidney's views on mimesis and poesis, as it is in the later play, rather than in _A Midsummer Night's Dream_, that Shakespeare attempts a thorough poetics of his magic art and indeed focusses all his dramatic perspective on that poetics. In the earlier play, artistic theory contributes to the action in an incidental rather than organic fashion; Shakespeare was obviously aware of the various positions it was possible to take, but awareness of the critical controversies sketched here does not affect the lightness of his touch.

The fairies of _A Midsummer Night's Dream_, like the authors of sixteenth and seventeenth century romantic comedy, create not the illusion of "real," that is, continuous time and space, but by illusions, create unnatural temporal and spatial discontinuities. The fairies turn the clock back to correct inequities, and forwards, either to make mischief, or in error. Transformations of individuals might be sufficient testimony of the method for any other playwright, but Shakespeare endorses Hippolyta's view that the collective witness is even more convincing. He therefore juxtaposes several magicked love affairs to foreground his play on time and to insinuate small differentiating factors between artistic and magic power.

A few examples may illustrate the point. Comparisons of the male lovers and Titania under enchantment are ordinary, if not odious; it is less often noticed that the women also look like Titania. Helena describes Demetrius as a "monster" (II.ii.96); the word acquires retrospective weight as Titania's situation is made analogous to Helena's by Oberon. Helena sees her pursuit of Demetrius as an inversion of the normal rules.

> the story shall be chang'd:
> Apollo flies, and Daphne holds the chase.
> (II.i.230-31)

Helena's unease reflects Athenian decorum, which subdues Amazonian behavior as fast as possible: "We cannot fight for love, as men may do" (241), as Theseus does, wooing Hippolyta by the sword. Oberon, implicitly agreeing with Athens, arranges to correct Helena's situation by magic. "Thou shalt fly him, and he shall seek thy love" (246).

114

Almost at once, however, Oberon uses the same magic to put his wife in Helena's predicament, and even improves on the job, allying royal (etymologically, real) womanhood with literal monstrosity. Oberon's power works in conflicting directions, towards and away from "normalcy," constructively towards a better future for Helena (a future that restores the past when Demetrius loved her), and destructively with Titania, pushing her back into the condition just left by Helena. Advance in one arena is checked by retreat in another.

Oberon presumably does not see the similarities between the enchanted Titania and abused Helena. This hint of a limit on his understanding is enlarged when, against all his expectation, Hermia joins the regiment of women pursuing monstrous men. Oberon, only part-controller of the play's action, does not stand wholly outside the situations he contrives, and does not fully frame our perspective on his actions.

If we required further evidence that Oberon cannot put a foot forward without also taking a step back, the fiasco that develops from his attentions to Lysander and Demetrius would offer proof positive. The fairies' will to correction only compounds the problems; instead of turning Demetrius' false love to true, the forest adds one more to its list of misalliances. Lysander is nearly indistinguishable from Demetrius. Lysander's outspoken

reluctance to harm the woman he no longer loves
(III.ii.269-70) rhetorically reflects Demetrius' would-be
virtuous veiled threats against Helena's person in Act II:
potential violence in each case succeeds the cease of love.
And, waking under enchantment, the two men virtually repeat
one another's lines. Compare Lysander's" And run through
fire I will for thy sweet sake!" (II.i.102) with Demetrius'
overblown rhetoric:

> O Helen, goddess, nymph, perfect, divine!
> To what, my love, shall I compare thine eyne?
> Crystal is muddy ... . (III.ii.137-39)

Magic correction and error have the same appearance.

But there is one crucial difference. Time divides these
two lovers; Lysander and Demetrius do not synchronize their
follies. Lysander, during the play, catches up with
Demetrius' inconstancy, which antedates the play. The
fairies' error replaces Demetrius with Lysander as the
latest Apollo to chase the wrong (and unappreciative) woman.
Eventually the fairies correct their own mistakes; if the
original magic both reverses and compounds error, the
antidote, at least, only corrects. But the damage to the
fairies' reputation is not so easily undone. Shakespeare
has created an irrevocable comic uncertainty about the
competence of magicians to prevail over time; they are
forced to put the clock back more than they intend, first,
by pushing Lysander into the position Demetrius takes before
the play begins, and second, by replacing Demetrius in the

116

situation he occupied even prior to that one, that is, before he met Hermia and switched amatory allegiances. Each deliberate magic change is countered by another, unwilled one, and the net result is, peculiarly, no change. The longer the fairies busy themselves about the lovers' affairs, the closer the lovers approach their original configurations.

Thus Shakespeare begins to disclose the hand behind the magicians, to indicate temporal manoeuvers for which the explicitly dramatized magic forces are not fully accountable. The fairies are not fully cognizant of and therefore do not completely control the temporal dimension in the wood. Nor, of course, do they quite rule its space. To begin with, their effectiveness depends on the accidental, which is to say externally contrived, convergence of lovers and artisans at the Duke's Oak, "near the cradle of the Fairy Queen" (III.i.74). Here the artisans meet to rehearse, "a mile without the town" (I.ii.94-95). The spot sounds oddly like the place Lysander pinpoints for his rendezvous with Hermia, "a league without the town" (I.i.115). And both lovers and artisans plan to meet "tomorrow night" (I.i.164). It seems that virtually the entire cast of the play heads for the same place at the same time. They engage in not merely analogous but coincident and coexistent actions.[28] Independent stories do

[28] Oxford English Dictionary defines "league" as not necessarily but occasionally equal to a mile. The folkloric

117

not just play themselves out concurrently; they enact themselves in the same theater on the same night, and moreover, occur as if by magic in the same represented space and represented time.

Shakespeare is asking us to see not an identification between physical stage and the place it represents, but on the contrary the fictiveness of such identification. Jorg Hasler notes a similar manipulation of stage and place at III.i.:

> The basic technique of word-scenery is here reversed. Quince is being demonstrative at the wrong moment. When he decrees that "This green plot shall be our stage, this hawthorn brake our tiring-house," he must point at the stage on which he stands, and at the tiring-house at the back of the stage -- the latter point being unfortunately lost in a modern theater. It is an "accident" that is likely to happen when we are shown not just a play-within-the-play, but also the work that goes into the shaping of its performance. The palace woods of Athens is gone in a flash; the basic illusion of A Midsummer Nights Dream is suspended.[29]

Shakespeare's suggestion from Act I onward is that we disregard the rational conclusion of our experience that successive scenes cannot represent independent unconnected actions (a lover's rendezvous, mechanicals' rehearsals)

---

tonality of the story and the fluid topography of the forest combine to suggest the virtual identity of the two places. On merely analogous actions see of course F. Fergusson, The Idea of a Theater (Princeton: PrincetonUniv. Press, 1949),e.g. p. 105.

[29] Hasler, Shakespeare's Theatrical Notation, pp. 82-83.

118

occurring at the same time and same place. We can cope with "Meanwhile back at the ranch"; "Meanwhile, in the same place" offers certain difficulties, and an interesting (at the very least) variation on the traditional unities.[30] Sequence has been replaced by a very special kind of discontinuity which is logically impossible, and more than merely fictive, a magical fusion, or in Agrippa's words, "knitting together," of something visibly distinct.[31]

The point is easily missed; the conventions of the bare stage, of romance, and of magic itself all condition the imagination to a habitual vagueness about precise detail. But insofar as the pains Shakespeare takes with detail are considerable, the question of his motive is legitimate. Why does he suggest a common ground for the performances of his artisans, lovers, and fairies? Most simply, of course, his aim is to satisfy theatrical conveniece and that tyrant, probability (or at least a pretence at probability, never one of Shakespeare's more pressing concerns in comedy). The

[30] It is tempting to view Shakespeare's technique here as a rebuttal to Sidney's objections to violations of the unity of place, cited above; Shakespeare's is unity of place with a difference.

[31] See Agrippa, The Philosophy of Natural Magic, pp. 39, 74-76, on magic's power to fuse disparate virtues; David Woodman, White Magic and English Renaissance Drama, p. 37, notes the logical if extreme conclusion to suspension of theatrical illusion in plays about magic, in quoting William Prynne's account of a performance of Faustus: the audience thought it could see "the visible apparition of the Devill on the stage at the Belsauvage Playhouse in Queen Elizabeth's day, to the great amazement of both the Actors and Spectators."

"marvellous convenient place" for the artisans rehearsal and the lovers' meeting is also convenient for the fairies; their collective convergence hear Titania's bower makes Oberon's and Puck's jobs much easier. Or at least, that is the idea. But in fact, though we might reasonably suppose that speedy globe-trotting fairies don't need this kind of authorial help, the reverse is true: place precipitates accidents in magic.

The fairies' magic depends on and is limited by events not of their making, and by spatial groupings of characters not of their choosing. Bottom's proximity to Titania, for example, plays into Puck's hands; the initiative for such arrangements rests ultimately, however, with the magicians' original, not with the fairies themselves. Bottom's vow, not to "stir from this place" when his friends run away from his newly forbidding features, shows signs of his own will as much as Puck's. The fairy, having translated Bottom, merely continues to exploit his presence; Puck is not responsible for the original placement of Bottom and indeed finds the proximity of hempen homespuns to a fairy queen rather surprising (III.i.73-74). The plans of Oberon himself are indefinite and vague, calling for the humiliation of Titania without spelling out the method.

The frivolity about Puck's ministrations likewise weakens any sense of economy and directedness in fairy strategy. Enjoying art for art's sake, Puck is clearly capable of translating Bottom just for fun; his expressed motive is artistic retaliation and one-up-man-ship over the artisans, whose performance he finds aesthetically offensive if admittedly amusing. Puck's capriciousness shines through his episodic narrative to Oberon. He recounts how he left "sweet Pyramus translated there" (III.ii.32) in order to pursue and misdirect the fleeing workmen:

> When in that moment, so it came to pass,
> Titania wak'd, and straightway lov'd an ass.(33-34)

The fairies make a virtue of necessity: obliged to rely on happenstance they exploit it with a will. Oberon's reply to Puck confirms Shakespeare's hints that the fairies are preeminently opportunistic: "This falls out better than I could devise" (35), he says, and it is better than Puck has devised, too.

Oberon's plans have to be indefinite enough to admit their adaptation to external necessity; fairy magic in A Midsummer Night's Dream is always contingent on existing temporal and spatial dispositions. The magic love-juice is both the agent and client of change, both the mover of and moved by circumstances. Its effectiveness is triggered by the waking of the sleeper, its results determined primarily by the proximity of a creature who may or may not arrive on the scene at tne fairies' behest. The exact degree of responsibility the fairies bear for the alarums and excursions that follow on the operation of the love potion

121

may seem unimportant for an audience to consider. But surely the actors need to have some ideas on the subject, if they are to represent rather than involuntarily to imitate the fairies' ignorance of limits on their power. Puck and Oberon both make mistakes they do not expect to make; actors, unable to avoid the wisdom of hindsight, have got to think through their parts from the characters' point of view, have got to decide what details the fairy does and does not arrange.

Shakespeare's portrait of Titania presents in more general aspect the confines of magic art.[32] Oberon's power to enchant her is significantly qualified; her vision is never completely subjugated to his direction. At the same time as she compliments Bottom on his wisdom and beauty she notes, albeit lovingly, the "mortal grossness" she plans to purge, so "That thou shalt like an airy spirit go" (III.i. 153-54). She seems to have a kind of double vision under enchantment, able at once to see Bottom's least fortunate deficiencies and yet to ignore them. "Tie up my love's toungue, bring him silently" (III.i.194), she prudently requests her servant. Titania presents, delightfully, both an object for ridicule and an exemplar of the very best kind of love, which falters not when faults appear in the beloved. It is characteristic of Shakespeare to endow

---

[32] Philip Edwards, Shakespeare and the Confines of Art (London: Methuen, 1968), pp.4-6, links artistic and magical power in his examination of Shakespeare's skepticism about his art.

figures of obvious absurdity with unwitting wisdom: Titania and Bottom are not entirely mismatched.

And so the joke is partly on Oberon. The magical transformation of Titania, like all magical transformations in the forest, is incomplete, contingent (on the accident of Bottom's proximity) and reversible. As we shall see, Shakespeare in The Tempest explores the reversibility of magic transformation through a more rapid, almost shimmering movement back and forth between physical and disembodied states; here in A Midsummer Night's Dream the surprise reversals take longer to accomplish, and are more overtly comic in tone. Oberon does not draw the obvious inference from the fairy queen's manifest susceptibility to magic: if Titania is subject to an enchanter's power, so also may Oberon be to another enchanter, the creator of Bottom. When Titania coos at Bottom: "Out of this wood do not desire to go," we do not laugh merely because the picture is incongruous, but because there is not the least likelihood of Bottom's imminent departure. And this is not just a result simply of arrangements made by Puck and Oberon, but of Bottom's own complaisance. He has already expressed his firm intent not to stir one foot from the place. Amenable to any kind of treatment, Bottom is not precisely a difficult subject for an enchanter; yet his self-possession robs the fairies of complete dominion over him.

123

And when the fairy king enters just after Titania leaves with her lover, he, Oberon, is still in ignorance about the results of his plot. He does not know to what his queen has awoken, "Which she must dote on in extremity" (III.ii.3). Immediately the risks inherent in Oberon's strategic indefiniteness are exposed in the revelation of Puck's mistake. The entry of Demetrius and Hermia prompts opposite identifications by Puck and Oberon: Puck realizes that"this is the woman, but not this the man," and Oberon discovers the opposite. Puck, having misinterpreted the decorous distance separating Lysander and Hermia earlier, has identified them as the Athenian couple (Demetrius and Helena) that Oberon ordered him to reconcile with the love-juice. The fairy is doubly confounded, first by the fact of an extra, unforeseen couple in the woods, and second by Helena's arrival in Lysander's vicinity at the very moment when, newly anointed, he awakes. Her almost miraculous appearance on the scene (she has successfully followed Lysander and Hermia even while they themselves were getting lost) precipitates the process in which the fairies' control over their own theater of operations is gradually, but spectacularly, diminished.

For Puck's original mistake seems to perpetuate itself before his astonished and uncomprehending eyes, and before the eyes of his disapproving master. Oberon's failures as supervisor undermine his credibility more seriously than he

124

undermines Titania's. She is allowed to make her mistakes flamboyantly, having them thrust upon her. Though Oberon, like Titania, is the victim of an authority outside himself, in his case that authority never identifies itself to him. Oberon's errors seem paradoxically more his own achievement than are Titania's, because he cannot trace them to their source, and she eventually can. The first accusation Oberon levels at Puck discloses the first inklings we have of Oberon's several omissions. Loosely, negligently commanding the forest, and unaware of the existence of Lysander and Hermia, Oberon has inadequately briefed his minion for the night's work. He then blames Puck for the error which only Oberon can recognize, and only _does_ recognize at this moment of recrimination, when he sees Demetrius in love with Hermia:

> Of thy misprision must perforce ensue
> Some true love turn'd, and not a false turn'd true.
> (III.ii.90-91)

And Oberon's righteous indignation on Lysander's part is, in any case, inconsistent with his willingness to turn true love to false for Titania.

The fairy king immediately sets about correcting his mistake. He directs Puck to find Helena and bring her "By some illusion" (98) to this place, while he charms Demetrius' eyes in readiness for her reappearance. Having failed signally, so far, to follow Helena's movements through the forest, the fairies now reveal themselves

125

capable of the task, when it is brought to their attention. But almost immediately Shakespeare gives a final, and very funny, turn of the screw against Oberon's energetic attempt to reestablish his will: Oberon witnesses Lysander (whose face he has never seen before) pursuing Helena. Unable to identify Lysander as the true lover turned false as a result of Puck's parallel failure of recognition eearlier, Oberon accuses his helper a second time:

> This is thy negligence: still thou mistak'st,
> Or else committ'st thy knaveries wilfully.
> (III.ii.345-46)

But Puck has actually only made one mistake: all the confusions follow on the single act of anointing Lysander instead of Demetrius. And it is Oberon's negligence as much as Puck's that allows the initial error.

That error appears to proliferate. Shakespeare demoralizes his magicians (though always lightly) by inducing in them a sense that their mistakes, and mistaking (not recognizing), have become an autonomous process that has taken on a life of its own. Since Oberon and Puck realize only belatedly that there are two pairs of lovers, and that only one pair exhibits trouble and strife, the momentum of events is no lonver in the fairies' control. The fairies share the lovers' inability to recognize which lover is which. The situation, to provide the graphic summary this play always seems to impose on its critics, moves as follows (arrows indicate direction of affection):

1. Before Puck anoints Lysander:   2. After Puck anoints Lysander:

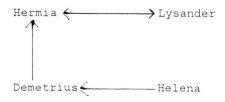

3. After Oberon anoints Demetrius:   4. After Oberon gives antidote to Lysander:

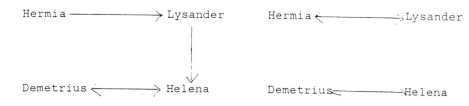

Oberon's operation in the third situation (3) creates a triangle exactly congruent with that of the first situation (1). The fairy solution of the puzzle posed by geometrical relationships in the play is retarded by the presence of two variables instead of one. There are two of everything: two women, two men, and two fairies overseeing the action. Oberon's two accusations are based on two interpretations, and indeed two consequences, of one original error: the first accusation, at III.ii.88, reflects Oberon's realization that Hermia is not the woman he saw before with Demetrius, and his second accusation, at III.ii.345, marks his discovery that Lysander is not the man he saw before with Helena.

But Shakespeare, never less than merciful, protects his Oberon from the consequences; however misjudged Oberon's self-styled superiority to Puck, the fairy king's dignity is unimpaired; Puck's lapses in concentration make him the scapegoat for his master's weaknesses. The fairy king is simultaneously dethroned, as it were, by his fai 'res, and allowed to continue unchallenged in office; A Midsummer Night's Dream is a particularly well-tempered comedy, and laughter gives back with one hand what it removes in the other.[33]

It is therefore in a context of comic irresolution that we should see the debilitation of the fairies' power. This is heralded by nothing grimmer than the approaching dawn: with their time running out, Oberon and Puck, whatever their differences, agree on the need for haste. The forces of magic are free to move "swifter than arrow from the Tartar's bow" (III.ii.101), but they are constrained to take full advantage of that gift for speed. Magicians' haste contrasts sharply with courtiers' enforced idleness. Through all the tedium of Bottom's "brief play," and despite universal impatience, Theseus continues to advise the court that "We must stay the time" (V.i.243). Nothing could indicate more graphically the incompatibility between Athens and forest, court and magicians, than their opposite tempi.

[33] Not all critics agree: for darker readings see e.g. Michael Taylor, "The Darker Purpose of A Midsummer Night's Dream," SEL, 9(1969),259-73.

128

Oberon cautions his aides, at the end of the play, to "Make no stay" in their flight through Athens: the fairies are not, after all, at home there.

Arguments for the conjunction between and interpenetration of Oberon's and Theseus' world at the end of the play generally tend to rest on the assumption either that the fairies are present on stage during most of the last act (and the artisans' play) or that they could be if they wished, and, if they wished, could cap all the artisans and courtiers lines.[34] The fairies, in other words, are in some way thought to achieve a kind of immanence in the action of Act V, by virtue of their (it is said) demonstrable transcendence over it. Thus David Young writes:

> In A Midsummer Night's Dream, this process of
> discovery reveals that the opposing worlds seem to
> form concentric circles. At first, following the
> characters from Athens to the woods, we may feel
> that the two areas are simply adjacent, but as
> Theseus and daylight reenter the play, we realize
> that it is possible to enter the woods and
> reemerge on the other side into human society.
> Thus, Theseus and his world seem to envelop the
> world of the woods. But Oberon and Titania, as we
> learn early in the play and are reminded directly
> at the end, are not the subjects of Theseus.
> Their awareness exceeds his, and their world is
> larger, enveloping his; he is their unconscious
> subject. Thus we discover another and larger
> circle, enclosing the first two. Then comes
> Puck's epilogue, which reminds us that everything
> we have been watching is a play, an event in a
> theater with ourselves as audience. Here is a

---

[34] See e.g. Edwards, Shakespeare and the Confines of Art, p. 56.

129

still larger circle, enveloping all the others.[35]

But in actual fact the fairies enter the last act after the artisans finish their play (according to the stage direction in both quarto and folio editions). The fairies' immanence in the action is easily overestimated. The magicians of the play do not fully control the last act; the two worlds nearly, but do not completely, penetrate one another. The disjunctions between them, which appear ever more prominently as the sway of magic over Athens is attenuated, have not been sufficiently stressed.

I have already described the brief hiatus or cesura between the recessional of Oberon at IV.i.101 and the entrance of Theseus at 102. The complete mutual obliviousness of the two groups presents two independent worlds, dramatically disjunct. Yet these mutual exclusives occupy virtually the same space at the same time. Shakespeare here, most clearly, renders a motif that is pervasive in the play, the colliding duplicates that create many of the play's disjunctions. The convergence of independent histories at IV.i.101-102 is closely analogous to the efforts of lovers and artisans, playing out their individual destinies, as if by magic, at virtually the same place and time. Only practical theatrical constraints, it would appear, prevent Shakespeare having concurrent

[35] Young, Something of Great Constancy, p. 91; succeeding references to Young are in my text.

130

renditions of successive scenes.

These duplicates are, essentially, discontinuities.[36] Critics who concentrate on the parallelism of theme that is afforded by Shakespeare's juxtaposition of scenes provide an indispensible service. But, as our familiarity with this manifestly Shakespearean strategy grows with the accumulation of criticism on the subject, we may lose our sensitivity to the strangeness of temporal progress and to the fracture of spatial integrity within and between scenes. Viewed sequentially, the juxtaposition of forest and Athens seems curiouser and curiouser, and always funnier, than it may from Young's avowedly atemporal, "spatial" analysis (p. 89). And the ample evidence of the last act's repeated efforts at closure testifies to Shakespeare's interest in sequential, temporal as well as static, spatial structures.[37] Distortions of sequence are often funny, and focus attention on sequence itself, and nothing disturbs sequence with quite the same force as repetition, duplication.

[36] See also Albert Cook, Shakespeare's Enactment, p. 26. For an alternative, psychoanalytic reading of the play's perceived duplicities, see e.g. Garber, Dream in Shakespeare, p. 73.

[37] Yet the tendency to "spatialize" time persists, in e.g. Gardner, "As You Like It," p. 22; Frederic Jameson, "Magical Narratives," The Political Unconscious: Narrative as a Socially Symbolic Act (Ithaca: Cornell Univ. Press, 1981), p. 112, describes romance time as "folds in space ... discontinuous pockets of homogeneous time and of heightened symbolic closure."

131

Much of the play's humor derives from the presentation of one set of characters inadvertently imitating the mistakes of another set. But our laughter is more accurately a function of our temporal sense than of some spatial conceptualization of the juxtaposition of like actions. Bergson appreciates the comedy involved in the <u>process</u> of imitation:

> We begin, then, to become imitable only when we cease to be ourselves. I mean our gestures can only be imitated in their mechanical uniformity, and therefore exactly in what is alien to our living personality. To imitate any one is to bring out the element of automatism he has allowed to creep into his person. And as this is the very essence of the ludicrous, it is no wonder that the imitation gives rise to laughter.[38]

The comic playwright, Bergson continues, extracts laughter through "the geometrical development" and "obvious clockwork arrangement of human events" (83), through, in other words, the replacement of life's natural rhythms with mechanical regularities. Bergson discounts the explanations of laughter as the "sudden dissolution of continuity" involved in suprise (86). But I think it is possible to argue that humor in <u>A</u> <u>Midsummer</u> <u>Night's</u> <u>Dream</u> depends simultaneously on the mechanical regularity with which, for example, each lover imitates the follies of his peers, and on the <u>unexpectedness</u> of such repetitions as imitation engenders.

---

[38] H. Bergson, "Laughter," in <u>Comedy</u>, ed. Wylie Sypher (Baltimore: Johns Hopkins Univ. Press, 1956), p. 81, with succeeding references in text; Langer qualifies Bergson's achievement, <u>Feeling</u> <u>and</u> <u>Form</u>, p. 117.

132

We do not expect people to behave like automatons, after all, with the predictability of machines. Shakespeare consistently exploits the element of surprise that duplicates and repetitions provoke. We have seen how the duplication of loving couples in the forest confounds the fairies and compounds the complications they would, in mischief, engineer. Ultimately the discontinuities of the play rest on the superimposition and sustaining of duplicate realities. The two worlds, of magic and reality, night and day, sit oddly with one another; the highest honors in the waking world clearly go to those who retain some impression of the magic and the dream. For Demetrius the forest seems only "As the remembrance of and idle gaud/Which in my childhood I did dote upon" (IV.i.165-67). The night's experiences appear to him now only dimly, something from a remote past and a remoter space: "These things seem small and undistinguishable/Like far off mountains turned into clouds" (186-87). Hermia's memory is clearer: the events of the night still superimpose themselves on her waking vision. "Methinks I see these things with parted eye,/When everything seems double" (188-89).

A true perception of the magic dimension involves not just the ability to see double, as Hermia can, but an appreciation of its strangeness.[39] Theseus, who dismisses

[39] Some critics attribute Brechtian Verfremdungseffekt to A Midsummer Night's Dream, e.g. Hasler, Shakespeare's Theatrical Notation, p. 83; Huston, Shakespeare's Comedies of Play, p. 98.

the lovers' stories as "more strange than true" (V.i.2), is contradicted by Hippolyta's "howsoever strange and admirable" (V.i.27). The women, if we recall Titania as well, seem more sensitive than the men of the play to double vision, and the surprises of the duplicate. An analogous alertness is required of us; an awareness of the independence of the play's two worlds is as necessary as an appreciation of their contiguity, and their points of continuity. The play requires considerable feats of memory from its audience.

Yet this is particularly difficult: one of the play's best paradoxes lies in the use of magic to induce sleep and forgetting. Demetrius' inferior sensitivity to the strange magic of the night (comparing him with Hermia) actually reflects a greater subjugation to the magician's last spell. Oberon, it will be remembered, finishes his sequence of enchantments with a spell that induces heavy sleep and amnesia in all the lovers (IV.i.67-68.80-81). Thus Lysander, on waking, cannot explain the new "gentle concord" (IV.i.142) wrought during the night, and Demetrius knows not by what power his love to Hermia "Melted as the snow" (IV.i.165); the spell for amnesia seems to work less effectively on Hermia, who thus, oddly, appears less susceptible to Oberon's power while simultaneously more sensistive to magic.

134

In the end, though, distance from the fairy magicians may lend them a greater enchantment. The power of this play's magic seems, curiously, greatest as the fairies' power diminishes. The play has, by Act V, conditioned us to notice disappearance, sudden withdrawals of characters, vanishing scenes, and pageants fading into airy nothings. The end of A Midsummer Night's Dream suggests that the whole play has in fact never really happened. Shakespeare does to us what Oberon does to the sleeping lovers: the enchanter's final spell is to make the night's accidents seem "But as the fierce vexation of a dream" (IV.i.67-68). For we realize, at the end of the play, that all the magic and all the night's accidents have in reality changed nothing. Demetrius now loves Helena -- as he did before the play began. And there is even more to it than this.

For the end of this comedy is, most oddly, implicit in its beginning. On the morning of May Day, in IV.i., Theseus and Hippolyta, entering the woods in observance of the traditional rites of May morning, naturally assume that the sleeping lovers have been doing the same thing. Theseus says:

> No doubt they rose up early, to observe
> The rite of May; and hearing our intent,
> Came here in grace of our solemnity. (IV.i.131-33)

Now Theseus, I think significantly, seems temporarily to have forgotten the discord and disturbances that plagued the lovers in the play's first scene. Perhaps he knows that

135

they have collectively observed the rites of May before.
Certainly we know they have, for Lysander tells us, early in
Act I: the place he arranges for his meeting with Hermia, a
league without the town, is the exact same spot where he,
Hermia, and Helena met at least once before "To do
observance to a morn of May" (I.i.167). This spot is where
all the characters of the play converge, and where
everything begins to go wrong. There is a curious sense of
deja-vu about the collective awakening in IV.i. Demetrius
freely acknowledges his former love for Helena, and declares
his return to that condition: Theseus' inability
immediately to recall the strife of the opening (and the
possible sentence of death on Hermia) enhances the brief
suggestion by Shakespeare that the whole action of the play
thus far is insubstantial and ephemeral in its impact.

It is as though, for a few delerious seconds, all this
has happened before, but without the night's accidents. We
recall Theseus' word for the artisans' play in Act V: he
calls is an "abridgement"(39) and commissions it to shorten
the three hours' wait before bedtime. The artisans' play so
interests the court that the time passes more quickly than
any anticipates: "we this night have o'er watched" (352),
says Theseus, surprised that "This palpable-gross play hath
well beguil'd/The heavy gait of night" (353-54).
Shakespeare manages to intimate, in terms far more than
merely rhetorical, that his very unpalpable-gross play, the

136

<u>Dream</u> itself, is some such abridgement.[40]

We know of course, through watching the play, that our time is being filled, and filled with surprises. But by the time we reach Act V, the result Hippolyta hopes for, a sense that time has passed miraculously quickly, seems also to have been achieved. The end promised in the play's opening exchanges appears oddly fulfilled; we have been made to feel strangely as though we have not in fact spent any time at all in the watching of the play, because in some way it has not really happened at all.

Shakespeare persistently assaults the expectations his audience might reasonably bring to a comedy, consistently defying any attempt to foresee outcomes. Like all the characters of the play, we, aware of genre, anticipate endings; Shakespeare confounds all anticipatory moves, all expectations. The one thing we do not expect in the surprise-ending of comedy is a return to the beginning. The collective, cumulative enchanted show that is the entire play itself dissolves, as the magic by which the play works its changes seems to subvert itself. Change in this play is change back, constructive regression: if action in time normally proceeds continuously into an indefinite future, action in this play proceeds discontinuously into a distant past. Change, like the fairy magic that engineers it, is in

[40] Hasler, pp. 154-55, makes a similar point.

the end a dissolving illusion. Yet, as becomes even clearer in The Tempest, Shakespeare's own magic art is never more powerfully enchanting than when he pretends to disenchant us.

# Chapter V

Shakespeare's dissolving magic: The Tempest

Critics often remark the compelling austerity of The Tempest. L.C. Knights attributes the play's mysteriousness, and his own "difficulty in saying simply and clearly where (he) feels the play's greatness to reside," to its "spare ... notation, that only gets its effect when the reader or spectator is prepared to collaborate  fully to give apparently slight clues full weight."[1] Anne Barton traces The Tempest's power to its extraordinary combination of density and openness:

> Spare, intense, concentrated to the point of being riddling, The Tempest provokes imaginative activity on the part of its audiences or readers. Its very compression, the fact that it seems to hide as much as it reveals, compels a peculiarly creative response.  A need to invent links between words, to expand events and characters in order to understand them, to formulate phrases that can somehow fix the significance of purely visual or musical elements is part of the ordinary experience of reading or watching this play.[2]

---

[1] L.C. Knights, "The Tempest," Shakespeare's Late Plays: Essays in Honor of Charles Crow, ed. C. Tobias and P.G. Zolbrod (Athens: Ohio Univ. Press, 1974), pp.15-17.  I use the Arden edition (ed. F. Kermode) of The Tempest.

[2] Anne Barton, ed., The Tempest (Harmondsworth: Penguin, 1981), p. 19.

139

The play works its magic on our senses by depriving them,[3] making us fill the spaces within its dramatic texture, enlisting our imaginations in the service of the play's fabrication.

This chapter argues that magic and imagination are both put to work explicitly in the play's silences, unexpected transitions, and structural discontinuities.[4] The significant developments of The Tempest occur during interruptions of dramatic progress. Prospero's magic repeatedly inhibits the completion of action contemplated by other characters: he puts some to sleep, and stills the swords of others. Instead of action Prospero offers spectacular shows that appear out of nowhere and vanish just as abruptly: the tempest, banquet, and masque, all punctuations of action, are themselves interrupted.

The abruptness with which the shows materialize and dissolve into nothingness creates an effect of suspension between reality and illusion;[5] our eyes are made to focus

---

[3] So Coleridge, Ninth Lecture on Shakespeare and Milton, in Coleridge: Essays and Lectures on Shakespeare and Some Other Poets andDramatists (London: Dent, n.d.),p. 454, writes that The Tempest "did not appeal to any sensuous impression ... of time and place, but to the imagination."

[4] For an interesting general discussion of structural discontinuity in the romances see Barbara Mowat, The Dramaturgy of Shakespeare's Romances (Athens: Univ. of Georgia Press,1976), e.g. pp. 98-99.

[5] A.D. Nuttall, Two Concepts of Allegory (London: Routledge,1967), p. 142, notes that everything in The Tempest is half one thing and half the opposite: "This recurrent sense of ambiguity and suspension is extremely potent dramatically."

140

more and more on the instant of transition between substance and shadow, nature and art. It is the precise point at which "real" meshes with "unreal" that is the focus of Shakespeare's artistry in the shows of The Tempest, and that most eludes critical definition.[6] Magicians habitually seek the point of conjunction between real and unreal: the practitioner of sympathetic magic who constructs an imitation of what he lacks and desires is not unlike the artist who tries to transmute base nature into gold by constructing a second nature that imitates and improves the familiar first, "making things better than Nature bringeth forth."[7] Prospero, at once artist and magician, aims to redeem his fellows and himself through a series of shows that, increasingly, transfigure as well as imitate natural objects: the banquet, masque and tableau of the lovers at chess are all images of plenty or peace.

[6] Anne Righter, Shakespeare and the Idea of a Play (New York: Barnes and Noble, 1962), p. 192, finds this a unique and reprehensible confusion in Shakespeare, unlike Robert Egan, Drama Within Drama (New York: Columbia Univ. Press, 1975), pp. 1-14, who specifically disputes Righter's pessimism about the play.

[7] Philip Sidney, The Defence of Poesy, p. 108; C.L. Barber, Shakespeare's Festive Comedy, is perhaps the best known critic to link magic and imagination, pp. 139ff.; Robert Egan, Drama Within Drama, pp. 93-95, also finds the link between magic and art in the "control of reality through imitation" and the presentation of a believable "mimetic vision of the ideal"; on believability of the play's illusions see David Young, The Hart's Forest: A Study of Shakespeare's Pastoral Plays, (New Haven: Yale Univ. Press, 1972), p. 178.

141

I argue finally that the play's magic is most fully exposed when what we see dissolves like the tempest into the calms of I.ii.. It is the disappearance of the banquet that gives the courtiers early warning of a lesson to be learned; it is when the masque collapses that the lovers begin to fulfil the prophecies of the masque. It is when the play's magic dissolves that we are transformed into magicians.[8] Prospero's abjuration of magic occurs only after its miracles have been contained in the new and better nature it has made. The renunciation of magic draws us into the world of the play, and empowers our imagination to reach beyond what we know, and to discover our better selves.

We cannot analyze how the play's strong illusions work to integrate nature and art, without first recognizing the initially divisive strategy of magic. The magic of The Tempest divides in order to unite, as the rope in I.i. is both noose and salvation.[9] Prospero and Ariel, indeed, always begin by interrupting some projected movement of events in time, or of bodies in space, arresting and

---

[8] For alternative, less positive views of the renunciation of magic see e.g. Andrew V. Ettin, "Magic into Art: The Magician's Renunciation of Magic in English Renaissance Drama," TSLL, 19 (1977),268-93; for a less consistently pessimistic reading see Howard Felperin, Shakespearean Romance, (Princeton: Princeton Univ. Press, 1972), pp. 247 ff.

[9] Neil Wright, "Reality and Illusion," p. 249, makes this point.

redirecting the play's temporal progress. Prospero puts
Miranda to sleep in I.ii. after having at last recounted
their past history up to the present moment. The mariners
are also divided from their senses -- put to sleep -- this
time by Ariel. They, unlike Miranda, remain asleep for the
whole play. In II.i. Ariel puts to sleep all the courtiers
but Antonio and Sebastian (their greater turpitude requires
stronger and more direct magic, as we shall see).

The essentially restorative purpose of sleep in the play,
though functioning in the end like the reconstitutive sleep
of _Lear_ and _Macbeth_, works in _The Tempest_ at first purely
negatively: as always in this play, magic's reintegrative
purpose is initiated by an interruption. Time simply stops
for the sleepers: magic creates not the heightened
intensity of a dream state as in _A Midsummer Night's Dream_,
but a temporary death to the world around them: the
sleepers are subtracted for a time from the developing
action, taken out of play time. Other characters exploit
the time magically taken from the sleepers: Antonio plans
to use the moment vouchsafed him by the sudden descent of
the others "as by a thunder-stroke" (II.i.199) into
oblivion: "Th'occasion speaks thee" (202), he advises
Sebastian, and the opportunity solicits their attention.
But their nefarious plans are in turn arrested by Ariel.
Prospero, who "through his art foresees the danger" (292),
sends Ariel, "For else his project dies, -- to keep (the

143

courtiers) living." Ariel thus wakes the sleepers to the sight of Antonio's and Sebastian's drawn swords.

So far the interruptions of sleep are accounted for by Prospero's and Ariel's magic: even the more evil intentions of the wakeful are in turn inhibited by -- we have now been conditioned to assume -- magic. But closer examination reveals an unexplained curiosity in this scene. The villains' swords are halted a split second _before_ Ariel works his magic: they pause, inexplicably, for "but one word" as they draw swords. _The Tempest_ abounds with interruptions not overtly magical in origin. Repeated and multiplied, they acquire a mysterious significance for which no theory of hasty composition will adequately account.[10] Once we discover that these mysterious breaks in continuity are rationalized elsewhere in the play by magic (as when Ferdinand's sword is halted), we begin to suspect that magic may occasionally work independently of the magician, and that Prospero's disrobing, "Lie there my Art," does not necessarily deprive magic of its power, but just denudes the magician of his.

When Prospero stills Ferdinand's sword, he also charms him from moving: implicit in the arrest of time is the halting of movement in space, as swords and sword-bearers are transfixed. Other magical interventions, by Ariel

[10] For a good example of textual and theatrical explanation of the play's interruptions, see Irwin Smith, "Ariel and the Masque in _The Tempest_," _SQ_, 21 (1970), 213-22.

144

particularly, break through the normal boundaries of place and person. In III.ii., for example, the lowest caste of villains, Caliban, Stephano and Trinculo, is repeatedly interrupted in its plotting by the invisible Ariel. Functioning like Puck in A Midsummer Night's Dream, III.ii., the spirit imitates in turn the voices of the conspirators. Caliban hears Ariel's "Thou liest" (44) and thinks Trinculo has spoken; similar interruptions occur twice more (61,73). Trinculo is threatened by Stephano with dire consequences should he "interrupt the monster one word further" (67), but of course he has not done so in the first place. Here the intrusion of the spirit Ariel into the private space of the villains is in truth an invasion and occupation of their persons. They are, as it were, not the same villains, their very physical integrity violated by the magic that reduces their power to act.

Magic inhibits the completion of action by interrupting the regular flow of time and space. But the induction of sleep and the stilling of swords do more than just introduce an artificially contrived break: Prospero amends his subjects by influencing their vision, not by directly conditioning their actions. He does not make them act; he lets them see, by offering shows or visions that are imitations of "real" situations, and the "real" time and space, to which the courtiers are accustomed.

145

The island itself, of course, is an imitation of real space. It is _like_ the real island of Bermuda, but _not_ Bermuda. Shakespeare presents its immateriality and indefiniteness as grounds, almost, for our belief in it. The island, like Prospero's magic shows, is an imitation of the real thing, except that its location is undefined. Shakespeare makes considerable issue of the fact that it is specifically not Bermuda, which was also renowned for tempests and enchantments[11] where Ariel fetches the dew necessary for the operation of magic. In view of Shakespeare's established use of Strachey's "True Reportory" of the shipwreck off Bermuda (1609) for details of the description of his island, it seem unlikely either that he was confused about, or that he intended to confuse, his fictitious island with the real one: he was familiar with the three main contemporary pamphlets about Bermuda,[12] Shakespeare's patron Southampton was one of the company of

[11] See Kermode's annotation to I.ii.229.

[12] William Strachey, "A True Reportory of the Wreck and Redemption of Sir Thomas Gates, Knight, upon and from the Island of the Bermudas," and Silvester Jourdain, "A Discovery of the Bermudas, Otherwise Called the Isle of Devils," both of 1610, and both in A _Voyage to Virginia in 1609: Two Narratives_, ed. L.B. Wright (Charlottesville: Univ. Press of Virginia, 1964); and the Council of Virginia's "A True Declaration of the Estate of the Colonie in Virginia" (1610) in _Tracts and Other Papers_, vol.3, ed. Peter Force (Washington: Peter Force, 1836-46); Strachey was not published until 1625, but was almost certainly read by Shakespeare before he wrote _The Tempest_, and scholars agree on his familiarity with the voyage; see e.g. Henry C. Wilkinson, _The Adventurers of Bermuda_, second ed.(London: Oxford Univ. Press, 1958), pp. 43-47; and Kermode, Arden ed., pp. xxvii-viii.

146

Virginia Adventurers which subsequently bought the Bermudas, and other acquaintances of Shakespeare had interests in the Virgina plantations including Pembroke and Lord De La Warr who became governor of the colony. It is even possible that Shakespeare met Strachey through friends of Thomas Gates.

Thus Shakespeare focusses our attention on the status of the island's reality. Antonio, responding to Gonzalo's inadvertent confusion of Tunis with Carthage, asks derisively "What impossible matter will he make easy next?" (II.i.85), sarcastically commending Gonzalo's error over the raising of the walls of Thebes (by Amphion's music): "His word is more than the miraculous harp" (83-84). Their dismissiveness actually lodges the Ovidian reference more firmly in our minds, and their skepticism suspends our disbelief in the power of imagination to construct place: Sebastian's suggestion that "I think he will carry this island home in his pocket, and give it his son for an apple," and Antonio's reply, "And, sowing the kernels of it in the sea, bring forth more islands" (II.i. 86-89), ironically raise the possibility their irony would deny. The interchange connects physical substance with imaginary space, and conveys a heightened significance to the negative geographic reality of Prospero's island. A place that is nowhere, it becomes, curiously, the more "real" to us as it is fictive: at any rate we can dismiss Morgann's censure of the play for _not_ being set in Bermuda as a perspective that is as inadequate as Antonio's and Sebastian's.[13]

The island, as an imitation of reality, allows the courtiers an artificial, or at least miraculously won, space and time in which to develop new and better capacities for action. But if the art of Shakespeare simultaneously figures and transfigures reality, imitating the natural world in order to improve human nature, so does the magic of Prospero. The Tempest visions, like the island, enact themselves on the borderline between real and unreal, substance and illusion. The tempest in which the ship is apparently "Dash'd all to pieces" (I.ii.8) and sunk appears to Miranda to have drawn the courtiers into a watery grave, merging them with the sea itself. She notices that the tempest blurs the boundary between sea and sky: "the sea, mounting to th'welkin's cheek,/ Dashes the fire out" (I.ii.4-5). It is as though the sea engulfs everything else, as though all were dissolved in it. Yet the tempest is a product of art, of Prospero's magic, which has "twixt the green sea and the azur'd vault/Set roaring war" (V.i.43-44); the tempest that dissolves everything in itself is itself a dissolving show, an artistic and magic illusion that the following scene explodes.

[13] Maurice Morgann, "A Commentary on The Tempest," in Maurice Morgann: Shakespearian Criticism, ed. Daniel A. Fineman (Oxford: Clarendon Press, 1972), p. 292.

148

The <u>Tempest</u> world hovers constantly on the edge of immateriality as well; the play's action consists largely in the swift crystallizing and dissolving of its magic visions that, like the spectacle in Friar Bacon's glass prospective, are as provocative as they are things of nothing. Interfering with dramatic momentum, Shakespeare's (and Greene's) shows recondition the audience's seeing in direct proportion as they fade away; the evanescence of the tempest, banquet, and later the masque, proves the insubstantiality of what is seen, and thus suggests that the visions are only real either in the magician's mind or, ideally, if he is successful, in the imagination of his audience.

And it is Ariel, subject to Prospero's supervision, who is master of these ceremonies, presenting both in name and deed the epitome of the play's instantaneous transitions and magic disembodiments. An airy spirit, whose physical virtuosity in space outdoes even Puck's, Ariel can merge at will with any of the four elements through which he travels,

<pre>
                                    be't
     To swim, to dive into the fire, to ride
     On the curl'd clouds. (I.ii.190-92)
</pre>

Ariel is thus ideally suited to present magical dissolving pageants. He is always in transit between two states of being. Bridging the elements, he is liquid air: "I drink the air before me, and return/Or ere your pulse twice beat" (V.i.102-103).

149

Ariel's ability to fuse the four elements confuses the sensory perceptions of his victims, and as we have seen, sensory deprivation initiates much of the play's magic. The source of the music that draws Ferdinand bodily nearer Miranda is Ariel, but is invisible: "Where should this music be?" queries Ferdinand, "i'th'air or th'earth?" (I.ii.390) The *Tempest* world is a place of sounds for which there is no visible source, and audible sights. The banquet appears suddenly in front of the courtiers, to the strains of "Solemn and strange music" (s.d. III.iii.17-18): it disappears just as suddenly to the accompaniment of thunder and lightning, reminiscent of the tempest scene itself. The visual discontinuity is aurally imaged by the sounds of a storm; and storms in this play indicate physical disturbance and discrete occasion, meteorological and spiritual crises that punctuate time. The Latin *tempestas* was in fact understood in the Renaissance as meaning both time and weather.[14] The mutual interference of sound and sight, our measure of time (in music) and space (in plastic arts), in the tempest and the banquet, suspend us between real and unreal, and crystallize what Julian Patrick calls the unstable "middle states of romances."[15]

[14] Julian Patrick, "'The Tempest' as Supplement," in *Centre and Labyrinth: Essays in Honour of Northrop Frye*, ed. E. Cook, C. Hosek, J. Macpherson, P. Parker, J. Patrick (Toronto: Univ. of Toronto Press, 1982), pp. 165,178, notes this and quotes in support an entry in Thomas Thomas' *Dictionarium Linguae Latinae et Anglicanae* (London: 1606).

[15] Patrick, "'The Tempest' as Supplement," pp. 163-64.

150

The disappearance, for example, of the banquet and shapes that present it and that "heavily vanish," is interrupted by Ariel's minatory speech, which is something complexly half-way between play-acting and honest truth. Ariel's vanishing is as noticeable as that of the shapes: putting on his own show, he describes Prospero by implication as a Fatal Power, for whom Ariel *et al* are ministering spirits. Ariel pronounces a lingering curse on the courtiers; all his prognostications for their future are half-truths, neither wholly real nor unreal estimates of the dramatic situation that Prospero has planned. Ariel's irruption into the vanishing scene divides the disappearance of the banquet from the exit of the shapes, and thus focusses attention on the business of vanishing (while practically providing the distraction necessary for a complicated piece of stage business). Ariel presents an internal discontinuity, interrupting the interruption, as it were. Shakespeare has made sure that the vanishing will indeed be heavy; the moments of poise between successive instants are weighted not only by what Ariel says, but when he says it.

And the significance of the culinary show has much to do with its sudden disappearance. The courtiers, who only realize the significance of this elusive magic when, much later, Prospero demystifies the event, are at this juncture understandably bewildered by what they have seen and heard: the more culpable of them (Alonso, Sebastian and an

151

unspecified "etc." in the stage direction) instinctively draw swords against the spirits, who, naturally invulnerable, make the swords more "massy" in a trice. Human activity is halted, and what Alonso and his train hear, see, and feel retains their attention primarily because they cannot understand it. What interrupts, also baffles: the shapes speak a silent and indecipherable message,

> Although they want the use of tongue -- a kind
> Of excellent dumb discourse. (III.iii.38-39)

Speech is only visible.

Inaudible speaking becomes a recurrent event in The Tempest. When Prospero and Miranda are on the way to Caliban to present him to us, Ariel returns briefly to receive a whispered, but unspecified, command from his master (I.ii.318). When Antonio and Sebastian briefly postpone the implementation of their homicidal ambitions for a word, that word is not divulged. These are not the accidents of rapid or incomplete composition, nor the result of a rough draft; the copy for the original 1623 Folio edition is unusually clean, and specific about stage directions, for example. We must assume that the recurrence of dialogue for which there is no script is deliberate.[16]

---

[16] Kermode, Arden ed., pp. xi-xiv; for more general estimates of the play's dumb discourse see W.T. Jewkes, "'Excellent Dumb Discourse': The Limits of Language in The Tempest," in Essays on Shakespeare, ed. Gordon Ross Smith (Univ. Park: Pennsylvania State Univ. Press, 1965), pp. 196-210; Gayle Greene, "'Excellent Dumb Discourse': Silence

152

Prospero, the supervisor and onlooker of the banquet scene, later on addresses "interlocutors" who are either absent or silent, in his apostrophe to the elves of hill etc., and to the courtiers who stand "spell-stopp'd" (V.i.33ff.) before him. Charmed and immobile in his magic circle, they have at last become a spectacle themselves, playing in dumb show and arrested movement to the magician himself. Prospero's magic dissolves sound in sight, hearing in seeing: the visible and invisible, corporeal and incorporeal, change place so rapidly and frequently in The Tempest that our sense perceptions are translated. We are taught to perceive, insensibly, what is not "really" there, to see what vanishes.

The greatest of the play's dissolving pageants is of course the masque of Ceres. Prospero explicitly connects it with the disappearing banquet, telling Ariel: "I must use you/In such another trick" (IV.i.35). Prospero's deprecatory posture on the subject of his art seems to invite contradiction, encourages us to endorse his magic. We mentally dispute Prospero's

               I must
       Bestow upon the eyes of this young couple
       Some vanity of mine Art. (141)

and Grace in Shakespeare's Tempest," Studia Neophilologica, 50 (1978), 193-205.

153

He would have us believe that magic is a thing of emptiness,
vanity if not vexation of spirit: but we have learnt to
value emptiness. The masque, though virtually without
action, is educative and ceremonial, information and praise
for the young couple whose betrothal it celebrates.[17] And,
as I shall show in the next few pages, the masque's full
meaning is revealed only in its effect on the lovers.

The masque takes us far deeper than before in the play
into unrealities and illusion. Its setting conflates times
and places even more than the play that contains it: we are
in some nowhere occupied at once by the goddesses of Greek
legend, near Cyprus and Paphos, and by the protégés of
Prospero. Venus, it seems, has been trying to inflict "Some
wanton charm upon this man and maid" (95). But all the
charms and bad magic of Venus and Cupid have, say the
masquers, been unable to prevail against the chastity of the
lovers.

Ferdinand's comment here, "This is a most majestic
vision, and/Harmonious charmingly" (118), is literally true:
the masque *is* a magic charm. Its actors are in "reality"
spirits, which Prospero's art calls to enact his present
fancies: they serve his imagination concurrently with his
magician's art. They are both the imaginative projections
of an artist's mind and the practical assistants of a

---

[17] My attention was drawn to the informing function of
Renaissance poetic encomium by Richard S. Peterson,
Imitation and Praise in the Poems of Ben Jonson (New Haven:
Yale Univ. Press, 1981).

154

magician.

Shakespeare stresses their spirituality rather than their actorliness. The direction of comparison is unusual: magic is not a species of playing so much as playing is a kind of magic.[18] We know of course that the actors who are spirits are in reality actors (we can see that they are) but what you see in The Tempest is not what you get, and vice versa. E.M.W. Tillyard's famous comment on the masque is still the clearest expression of Shakespeare's achievement:

> When we examine the masque, we find that, though its function may be simple, the means by which it is presented are complicated in a manner we associate rather with Pirandello than with the Elizabethan drama. On the actual stage the masque is executed by players pretending to be spirits, pretending to be real actors, pretending to be supposed goddesses and rustics,[19]

who are telling the story of their youthful audience. But in the end we have to remind ourselves of the spirits' actorliness (i.e. both their real identities as actors and their pretence at acting).

[18] See K. Berger, "Prospero's Art," Shakespeare Studies, 10 (1977), 213-15, and D. Woodman, White Magic, p. 80, on Ficinian magic: the Ficinian spirit, which Ariel and the masquers may represent, is the means by which magic reaches our imagination, and the spirit works its magic by artistic methods. Art serves magic, rather than the other way around.

[19] E.M.W.Tillyard, Shakespeare's Last Plays (1938; rpt. New York: Barnes and Noble, 1964), p. 80.

155

Interior plays in Shakespeare always enforce reflections on the fact and quality of theater, and usually establish the theater's power by insistence on its theatricality. Here, in The Tempest, though theatrical artifice is mentioned and the presence of actors is noted, their significance is accounted for in another way, by their participation in the operation of magic. Shakespeare in The Tempest dramatizes and extends the rhetorical claim of The Winter's Tale that the art that mends nature is nature, not merely, as in The Winter's Tale, because magic is natural, but also, as only The Tempest makes clear, because nature is magical. Agrippa, noting this, might be speaking of the Tempest world: "For every day some natural thing is drawn by art, and some divine thing is drawn by Nature, which, the Egyptians, seeing, called Nature a Magicianess, (i.e.) the very Magical power itself, in the attracting of like by like, and of suitable things by suitable" (pp. 123-24). In The Tempest version of metatheater, in its dissolving shows, theater calls less attention to itself than does magic, and theater ultimately seems to disappear;[20] Alvin Kernan has called The Tempest Shakespeare's "pure theater of the

---

[20] Anne Righter, Shakespeare and the Idea of a Play, p. 192, notes the absence in the romances of real theatrical terms like "cue" and "stage" and the substitution of play metaphors "inherent in the structure of the English language, the abstract 'scenes' and 'acts' of the early histories, stripped of reference to the London theatre and its particulars"; Shakespeare was not, as she thinks, turning his back on the theater but broadening art's frame of reference to include (and assimilate to) magic and the highest neoplatonic ideals.

156

imagination," "idealized theater," a "magical enclosure" or magic circle in which the playwright, unencumbered by physical, actual theatrical reality, has virtually unlimited powers.[21]

Shakespeare in the masque presents, for the first time in his career, _two_ simultaneous sources of illusion in the masque: magic and dramatic art. By pressing the claims of magic to a higher authority than that of any public theater or court drama, that is, by stressing that a magician, not a playwright, lies behind the masque, Shakespeare, through Prospero, makes an extraordinary and unprecedented case for the power that theater may, ideally (and the word is crucial) command. It is preeminently in the masque that Shakespeare aims to realize, through magic, a kind of neoplatonic Idea of theater, that is not a turning away from but a transfiguration of art into something literally magical. The masque is the only magic show that is seen from the beginning by those on stage to be illusory, yet it is this high artifice that gradually, and to an astonishing degree, suspends disbelief. Shakespeare asks us to believe in his illusions and his play not because they mirror our world, but because they idealize and can improve it.

[21] Alvin B. Kernan, _The Playwright as Magician_ (New Haven: Yale Univ. Press, 1979), pp. 133-34; the masque in the play is, as S. Orgel, _The Illusion of Power_ (Berkeley: Univ. of California Press, 1975), p. 45, notes, "not a real masque, but a dramatic representation of one."

157

And the masque is the center of the play's gravity. Our direction of vision is radically different from the customary orientation other interior plays tend to impose on us: we focus towards the masque instead of looking out from it to the play world beyond it.[22] In A Midsummer Night's Dream, for example, we see the internal play in Act V as a reflection of the external dramatic action; this reflection in turn bears on the "real" world beyond the playhouse. The fallibility of artisans reflects that of the lovers, courtiers, fairies, and in the end ourselves. The Pyramus play points outward, beyond itself. The masque of Ceres shows Ferdinand and Miranda themselves in quite different fashion. They see an ideal version of themselves (from which they are not, admittedly, far distant), the prior Idea of which they are the secondary physical reality. The masque does more than reflect their potential; it identifies it directly. The goddesses bring out the best in their audience, harmonizing information with praise. Like the practitioner of sympathetic magic, they help to create what they claim to see in the lovers. Miranda and Ferdinand are literally translated by Prospero's magic.

[22] See also R. Egan, Drama within Drama, p. 96: "Prospero does not emphasize to his audience the fictive nature of his images but attempts to substitute them directly for reality." The play's introspective structuring of illusions, what Nuttall, Two Concepts of Allegory, p. 146, calls its "regress of fictions," draws us within its unreality, focussing our eyes on its fiction.

Even more remarkable than the neoplatonic echoes is Shakespeare's audacious juxtaposition of the "real" and "Ideal" editions of the lovers together on one stage: the masquers, it is true, only tell of the lovers, and do not bodily represent them, but the implication is there. The artist-magician arranging and directing the masque can see the real forms of Ferdinand and Miranda at the same time as he watches his idea of what they should and will be in the masque: he need only turn his head. As if to confirm that implied juxtaposition, Shakespeare throughout the play suggests a strong analogy between parenthood and artistry: in Miranda, Prospero sees something that is doubly his creation, even without the masque. Tutored, formed and shaped by her father, Miranda is, as Jonson said of his son, his best piece of poetry. She is, like the other productions of Prospero's magic, a thing of wonder: her name indicates her function, which is to be admired, as a work of art is.

But like the other distillations of his magic, like the masquers, she is eventually active as well as passive. It is Miranda, "the created/Of every creature's best," who will later admire and endorse the marvels of the brave new world. She has moments of great psychological depth, as when she weeps

> At mine unworthiness, that dare not offer
> What I desire to give, and much less take
> What I shall die to want. But this is trifling,
> And all the more it seeks to hide itself,
> The bigger bulk it shows. Hence, bashful cunning!
> (III.i.77-81)

159

Like the Ferdinand she admires, who carries a brave form but is a spirit (I.ii.414), Miranda's personality and substantiality is a dramatic illusion, marvelous and shifting. Sometimes she seems human, as she weeps for her "sins," and sometimes she is the vehicle for an idea, and expresses in her person the state of being such a vehicle. Miranda, like all the other things of wonder in The Tempest, may seem most vividly impressed on our senses when she is least accessible to them, when least a bodily character, a tangible reality, and instead an idea, a wonder of art. The juxtaposition and mutual exchange of real and ideal on stage appears in the end to fuse them: Miranda embodies both nature and art.

Shakespeare manoeuvers us by degrees, as the play progresses, into seeing and then turning our backs on Sidney's distinction between the poet's mimetic fiction and reality itself, between the second nature of art and our own natural world. Wallace Stevens wrote that "Both in nature and in metaphor identity is the vanishing point of resemblance";[23] things that are are only alike, and not identical, must also by definition be in some degree different. Indeed Sidney's own departures from the Republic Book 10 (where poetry is denigrated as the imitation of an

[23] W. Stevens, The Necessary Angel (1951; rpt. London: Faber, 1960), p. 72, quoted by Righter, Shakespeare and the Idea of a Play, p. 192.

160

imitation),[24] in his neoplatonic belief in poetry's power to body forth the Idea rather than the mere brazen reality, actually polarize art and nature, the imitation with the real, still further. Shakespeare, like Sidney, seems to endow the art (in this case the masque) with a higher status than the natural reality itself. That the masque has some share in the lovers' improvement is suggested by the fact that it records what we do not see enacted on stage: we have seen the chastity test in progress, but we learn conclusively of their successful passage through it _during_ the masque. Shakespeare dramatizes and realizes Sidney's hope that the artist can teach as well as delight: the lovers are not translated into the artistic versions of themselves only by and during the masque, but assume that golden nature after it is over.

Prospero, we remember, regards the masque as a transforming event: he insists on silence not for the conventional theatrical reasons but so that the magic may work, so that the masque may run its crucial and appointed course:

> Sweet, now, silence!
> Juno and Ceres whisper seriously;
> There's something else to do: hush,and be mute,
> Or elso our spell is marr'd. (IV.i.124-27)

---

[24] Plato, _Republic_, Book 10, in _Critical_ _Theory_ _Since_ _Plato_, ed. Hazard Adams (New York: Harcourt, 1971), pp. 33-41.

161

The masquers do more than celebrate a "contract of true love." The masque actually cements natural forces of attraction, and the magic draws out and confirms natural sympathies (Ferdinand's and Miranda's mutual love): nothing else at this point can explain Prospero's anxiety that the masque be completed. If the masque dissolves the ordinary notion of theater and substitutes by magic the Idea of theater, it also performs the opposite function, drawing the "real" or brazenly natural world, the physically present lovers, into its fiction: Shakespeare has fused what Sidney implicitly polarized, as the second nature of art merges with the first nature of this world.

There is a brief doubt as to Shakespeare's and Prospero's success, as the masque does not run its appointed course. Prospero "starts suddenly and speaks" (s.d.IV.i.138-39) something we are not privileged to hear. Prospero's famous lines about the end of the revels seem to declare with absolute finality the fragility, unreality, and impermanence of art. But the power of Shakespeare's art is augmented as Prospero's deteriorates. The exchanges that follow the interruption of the masque demonstrate a Prospero who is, like his fellow characters, divided from himself, a fractured, fallible mortal. And where Prospero seems least in command of himself and of us, there we find Shakespeare in authority.

The great speech, when considered both in isolation and in its dramatic context, undermines its apparent intent. Here is what Prospero says:

> These our actors,
> As I foretold you, were all spirits, and
> Are melted into air, into thin air:
> And, like the baseless fabric of this vision,
> The cloud-capp'd towers, the gorgeous palaces,
> The solemn temples, the great globe itself,
> Yea, all which it inherit, shall dissolve,
> And like this insubstantial pageant faded,
> Leave not a rack behind. (IV.i.148-56)

Clearly Prospero speaks from the heart; yet his voice carries a resonance that is not fully in his command. The lines are far more than an expression of individual grief. Prospero is being occupied by and contained in a competing and ultimately higher authority. What then does <u>Shakespeare</u> mean to say? The speech does, of course, as Brower notes, invite a kind of constructive misreading:

> By the time we have passed through "dissolve," "insubstantial," and "faded," and reached "Leave not a rack behind," we are reading "cloud-capped towers" in reverse as a metaphor for tower-like clouds. "Towers," "palaces," "temples," "the great globe," "all which it inherit," are now taken for cloud forms. Through a sort of Proustian merging of icon and subject, we experience the blending of states of being, of substantial and unsubstantial, or real and unreal, which is the essence of <u>The Tempest</u> metamorphosis.[25]

But such imaginative integration of substance and shadow does not, in fact, seriously distort Shakespeare's meaning: it is Shakespeare who places the cloud-capped towers in

---

[25] Reuben A. Brower, "The Mirror of Analogy: <u>The Tempest</u>," in his <u>The Fields of Light</u>: <u>An Experiment in Critical Reading</u> (New York: Oxford Univ. Press, 1951), essay rpt. in <u>Shakespeare's Later Comedies</u>: <u>An Anthology of Modern Criticism</u>, ed. D.J.Palmer (Harmondsworth: Penguin, 1971), p. 424.

163

apposition to "the baseless fabric of this vision."

The claim that life is like a dissolving pageant is made en route to a more profound affirmation: it is by their very dissolution that such pageants are sustained, because it is in dissolving that they capture our imagination. The best description of the process is Kernan's:

> Prospero goes on to qualify his contempt for the impermanence of his art by reminding his listeners that while reality may seem to take immediate precedence over such "insubstantial pageants," reality is itself, finally, an illusion too ... It is a paradoxical triumph for art, in which the theater's illusory status, which had troubled Shakespeare for so long, becomes finally the source of the play's ability to mirror reality. Plays are not real, but then neither is the world itself.[26]

I would, further, emphasize that the magical art of The Tempest transforms both illusions, of art and life, into something positive; the play proves the argument of the sonnets that art translates, that is, imitates and redresses, the fading of the wide world's sweets. Sonnet 19 records the action of time as the action of a disfiguring artist.[27]

> O carve not with thy hours my love's fair brow,
> Nor draw no lines there with thine antique pen.
> Him in thy course untainted do allow,
> For beauty's pattern to succeeding men.
>    Yet do thy worst, old time; despite thy wrong,
>    My love shall in my verse ever live young.

[26] Kernan, The Playwright as Magician, pp. 144-45.

[27] I quote from Stephen Booth, ed., Shakespeare's Sonnets, (New Haven: Yale Univ. Press, 1977).

164

The rival artist (the rival of time) of the last couplet displays a defensiveness that belies the belief he expresses in the power of his art; the situation is virtually reversed with Prospero. His art, like time, disfigures, but also transfigures, and his pessimism acts, contrarily, to confirm our belief in its permanence.

If the dramatic context of Prospero's revels' end speech justifies skepticism about what Prospero _does_ say, the scene itself focusses our attention on what he does _not_ say. Prospero suspends the masque when the time, and his inner turmoil, interrupt his vision: remembering Caliban's conspiracy, he experiences a sudden intensified awareness of the time. "The minute of their plot/Is almost come" (IV.i.141-42), he asserts. His unprecedented "distemperature" combines temporal consciousness and emotional tempestuousness, yet this tempest of the mind, like that of the play's first scene, is if not exactly illusory at least quickly over; Prospero's own tempest subsides into the curious undirectedness and laxity of the minutes that follow.

For nothing in the subsequent dialogue convinces us that the magician's art is seriously threatened by the menacing reality outside his immediate circle. Instead of rushing off and dispatching the villains once and for all, Prospero takes time to meditate on it all. Everything about the next exchange is curiously divorced from direct purpose and

165

result. To start with, Prospero projects his disturbance onto the lovers without realizing how: he assumes Ferdinand is moved by the end of the revels, whereas, as we know, the lovers are more baffled by Prospero himself. Prospero's projection of his mood may of course reflect his own dismay at the cessation of the revels rather than his recollection of Caliban: but, and this is characteristic of the scene, we are not told one way or the other.

So, perhaps, Prospero recollects himself from the pleasureable contemplation of his art. His attempt to cheer Ferdinand up is easily read as an effort to cheer himself up, particularly since Ferdinand's reaction to the speech is never clarified, and Prospero's is: he remains vexed. He has not of course addressed the specific cause of his anger, which is the intrusion of Caliban upon his imagination, but voiced a more general apprehension of art's frailty. That in turn is wrongly attributed by Prospero to Ferdinand (and we never know if Prospero realizes the mistake). Prospero's real motives in this scene seem always disjunct from the ones he expresses.

The process continues. Prospero's authority has patently diminished, and he apologizes to Ferdinand:

> Bear with my weakness; my old brain is troubled:
> Be not disturb'd with my infirmity;
> If you be pleas'd, retire into my cell,
> And there repose: a turn or two I'll walk
> To still my beating mind. (IV.i.159-63)

166

Only now does he appear to realize that his mood may be as disturbing as the end of the revels. But the speech is, in part, a feint. Prospero leaves Ferdinand not just to be alone and pull himself together, but more specifically to complete arrangements for the downfall of Caliban. The lines, carrying an unmistakeable ring of conviction, are a diversionary tactic: Prospero needs to get rid of the lovers to meet Ariel. What is going on here? Prospero's contribution to the scene recalls Ariel's strategic half-truths on the occasion of the disappearing banquet; he is not, as Ariel was not, the chief magician. Prospero's fragmented response to the collapse of his masque has, as Ariel's contributions to the banquet scene did, an improvisational quality that suggests that the magician's capacity to contain the action is being strained to breaking-point. Neither Ferdinand nor Prospero seems to comprehend the other's distress, and thus neither speaks quite to the point. This is surely the strangest defense of poetry ever written: but that is its ultimate effect; the magic is reconstituted. For when the magic show is interrupted, our imaginations must take over from Prospero's. Desire empowers both magic and imagination, and when Prospero appears to lose grip and coherence, forced to dissipate his energies over too wide a field, our imaginations are forcibly impressed in Shakespeare's business, constructing the the meaning of the scene by

167

filling in its curious gaps.  Shakespeare seems always to
work through surrogates:  and in this case we substitute for
Prospero.

The breaking off of the revels thus formally mirrors the
interruptive nature of the masque as a whole: both in
progress and in its dissolution it presents an image of the
interruptions by which Prospero's magic typically gets
results.[28] The masque appears as an interlude in the play
proper; the sense of interval is enhanced by its leisurely
rhythm.  The goddesses have relaxed their normal activity:
Iris tells Ceres that Juno wants her to leave her habitual
pursuits to come and sport, to entertain Juno.  The pace is
gentle, the contrast with the thunder and lightning of the
vanishing banquet just preceding, most pronounced.  The
shift recalls the progression from I.i. to I.ii.

The masque is both a hiatus and a magic spell intrinsic
to the play's meaning, harmonizing realities with ideals; it
suggests and bridges a break within the dramatic action.
When the Idea of the lovers in the masque has collapsed, it
is incorporated, embodied, in the characters on stage:  they

---

[28] On the transcience of the masque in the play see
e.g.  Frye, "Romance as Masque," in his Spiritus Mundi:
Essays on Literature, Myth, and Society (Bloomington:
Indiana Univ. Press, 1976), p. 158; Allardyce Nicoll,
"Shakespeare and the Court Masque," Shakespeare Jahrbuch, 94
(1958),59-60 thinks the revels' end speech refers to the
changeability of Inigo Jones's masque scenes; S. Orgel, "New
Uses of Adversity: Tragic Experience in The Tempest," in In
Defense of Reading: A Reader's Approach to Literary
Criticism ed. R. Brower and R.Poirier (New York: Dutton,
1962), p. 125 notes that the masque is "first of all an
interruption of the dramatic action."

168

still, after the masque, bear the marks of their translation into art. Masques usually present "a moment of transformation,"[29] and in The Tempest the masque is congruent with the lesser instants of transformation through the play: everywhere we see the mutual approach and sudden meeting of concrete realities and the insubstantialities of art. The masque, of course, dramatizes an extended moment of transformation, a longer display of the magic that divides and unites, and that finally reconciles antithetical states.

If the masque's position and shape mirror those lesser healing divisions within the structure of The Tempest, they all, equally, mirror the play as a whole, which presents in broad terms a moment of transformation in the lives of its characters, a complete break with their past and an entry into a hitherto unimaginable future. The five acts dramatize a much shorter duration than is usual in Shakespeare: a single afternoon. The Tempest enacts an analogous "gap" to the one for which Time apologizes[30] between Acts III and IV in The Winter's Tale:

Impute it not a crime

[29] F. Kermode, Arden ed., p. lxxiii.

[30] Quotation is as usual from the Arden edition of The Winter's Tale, ed. J.H.P.Pafford (London: Methuen, 1963).

> To me, or my swift passage, that I slide
> O'er sixteen years, and leave the growth untried
> Of that wide gap, since it is in my power
> To o'erthrow law, and in one self-born hour
> To plant and o'erwhelm custom.(IV.i.4-9)

The Winter's Tale dramatizes the characters' history before and after the sixteen year hiatus. The gap in The Tempest is actually twelve years, and also undramatized. But the later play turns the earlier inside out by giving us four hours on Prospero's island instead of the two sides of the temporal gap in The Winter's Tale. Whether or not The Tempest deliberately answers censure of violated unities in the earlier play, it is clearly a formal variation on it, compressing the first three acts of The Winter's Tale into Prospero's brief narrative exposition (I.i.) and expanding the last two acts of The Winter's Tale into five.

The Tempest also realizes a metaphorical suggestion of A Midsummer Night's Dream. As I noted in my chapter on that play, Shakespeare hints towards the end that the whole of the action in and around Athens from Act I may be viewed as an "abridgement" (Theseus' word for Bottom's play). Puck's closing advice to us to regard the play as a dream confirms our fleeting impression when the lovers awake on May morning, as they have collectively done before, that all the play's action has only reestablished a situation that existed prior to it, and that the action has been some kind of illusion. But the suggestion is not essential to the play's meaning: it merely enhances the magical atmosphere

170

the fairies and their author contrive. A Midsummer Night's Dream is only metaphorically an abridgement. The Tempest realizes the figure in far more concentrated fashion, bridging and dividing past and future more completely and more creatively than anywhere else in Shakespeare.[31]

The dramatic present of The Tempest, like that in most comedies, is both a break and a consolidation in the characters' histories; what distinguishes The Tempest is the intensity and resonance of its temporal interruption and reintegration. Like its internal masque, the play is actually about the transforming moment, about what happens in the instant between before and after. It is as though the normal structural disjunctions of romance and arbitrary twists of comic plots have become the focus of Shakespeare's art. The Tempest articulates (etymologically: divides and binds) the characters' spiritual progress. At the same time Shakespeare enables us to see the turning point of their history more clearly by extending our sense of the play's revolutionary present (and in real life the present is technically a point of no duration) into five acts. The result is a curiously mixed atmosphere, at once charged with

[31] Mowat, The Dramaturgy of Shakespeare's Romances, p. 104, speculates, with mixed success, that "the action on the island is a play-within-a-play," and that "Shakespeare has somehow turned us into the Theseus and Hippolyta-like audience of A Midsummer Night's Dream." Her argument rests on the now canonical assertion first made by Frye, The Anatomy of Criticism, (Princeton:Princeton Univ. Press, 1957), p. 185, that The Tempest takes place wholly in the green world that is the disordered middle state of his tripartite comic structure, and is framed by art.

171

a sense of crisis, yet also, strangely, static.

More immediately obvious is the play's dramatization of a critical present. Prospero's intuition of crisis confirms the significance of the play's first, tempestuous scene:

> By accident most strange, bountiful Fortune,
> (Now my dear lady) hath mine enemies
> Brought to this shore; and by my prescience
> I find my zenith doth depend upon
> A most auspicious star, whose influence
> If now I court not, but omit, my fortunes
> Will ever after droop. (I.ii.178-84)

Prospero asks the time at I.ii.239, at which point it is about 2p.m.: he specifies that "The time 'twixt six and now/Must by us both be spent most preciously" (240-41). The frequent reference to the time reflects not merely Shakespearean insistence on the unities but Prospero's own sense that his four hours are a vitally important occasion in his history. Miranda tells us that her father was often on the point of revealing the past to her, but the time was never ripe, and he always stopped short. However now he tells her that "The hour's now come;/The very minute bids thee ope thine ear" (I.ii.36-37). The other protagonists unwittingly share his insight: the occasion independently makes itself felt by all. Antonio recasts the notion in theatrical terms (one of the play's few overtly theatrical as opposed to artistic gestures):

> We all were sea-swallow'd, though some cast again,
> And that by destiny, to perform an act
> Whereof what's past is prologue; what to come,
> In yours and my discharge. (II.i.246-49)

172

It is not in their discharge, of course, as ultimately it is not in Prospero's. The drama of the present is its uniqueness: we, like Antonio and all the others, see as a rule only the transience, the fading reality, of the present we live through. The Tempest is that unrepeatable, disappearing, climactic instant, frozen into art. Even Caliban senses the singularity of the occasion: "we shall lose our time" (IV.i.247), he says, chafing at the frivolous delays of Stephano and Trinculo.

And the whole action of the play can be seen in a moment. Thus Gonzalo's recognition of Prospero's magic accomplishment, bursting suddenly from him, spontaneously recapitulates the action for us:

> O rejoice
> Beyond a common joy! and set it down
> With gold on lasting pillars: in one voyage
> Did Claribel her husband find at Tunis,
> And Ferdinand, her brother, found a wife
> Where he himself was lost, Prospero his dukedom
> In a poor isle, and all of us ourselves
> When no man was his own. (V.i.206-13)

What is by now only recapitulation for us is for Gonzalo a new discovery: yet his exuberant bid to translate his experience into something permanent (and interestingly, golden writing) carries us with him, and the effects of Prospero's magic are conjured up for us again, minus the frustrations he engineered: we rediscover our experience of the play. The general structure of The Tempest lends itself to narrative condensation because the stories are reducible

173

to a common denominator: all embrace their destinies when least themselves, when possessed by something greater, here, magic.

The terms in which Gonzalo couches his inspiration echo those of the other romances: the critical action in these plays literally takes protagonists out of themselves. So Pericles[32] asks Helicanus:

> put (me) to present pain,
> Lest this great sea of joys rushing upon me
> O'erbear the shores of my mortality,
> And drown me with their sweetness.(V.i.191-94)

Leontes is "ready to leap out of himself for joy of his found daughter" (V.ii.50-51). Discovery in the romances is like the process described by Whitehead:

> a broadening of feeling due to the emergence of some deep metaphysical insight, unverbalized and yet momentous in its coordination of values. Its first effect is the removal of the stress of acquisitive feeling arising from the soul's preoccupation with itself.[33]

The turning point of a romance is, as Kermode thinks, more accurately recognition than peripetia,[34] dreamily ecstatic

---

[32] _Pericles_, ed. F.D. Hoeniger (London: Methuen, 1963).

[33] Quoted in Dover Wilson, _The Meaning of_ The Tempest (Newcastle: Literary and Philosophical Society, 1936),p.22.

[34] Kermode, _The Final Plays_ (London: Longmans for British Council, 1963),p.11,rpt. in _Shakespeare, Spenser, Donne_ (London: Routledge, 1971); Walter F. Eggers, Jr., "'Bring forth a wonder': Presentation in Shakespeare's Romances," _TSLL_, 21 (1979), 455-77, argues two phases of wonder, first, emotional transport and loss of self awareness, and second, intellectual, which he feels is more significant in the plays.

174

rather than busily active.

The demonstrable sense of crisis through The Tempest is also peculiarly muted. The really dramatic effects of the play are achieved by deflating melodramatic possibilities, and deflecting proposed actions. The menace offered by villains bent on rape and murder is weakened and dulled well before the play's end: Prospero dampens their ardor for violence any time it threatens to become a significant influence on the action. Critics have often remarked on the absence of activity and suspense in the play. Michael Goldman writes:

> The action of the play is notably free from suspense or impediment, a fact that is made clear almost from the start. In a sense it is as if the last scene of The Winter's Tale were now taken as province for an entire play -- the formal slipping of a knot already not only loose but unfastened, under the control of a powerful benign enchantment. The quality of enchantment is central, and that is why the atmosphere is primary. The play's events are less important than the way they are felt: how they are received by the characters, how they appear to us, and how they are related to the arts of theatrical illusion in general.[35]

It is not just that the projected crimes come to nothing: they are not felt, except by Prospero, as serious threats, and his responsibilities entail suffering and anxiety that we do not share. We see his unease at the end of the masque but do not know precisely how and why he is burdened.

[35] M. Goldman, Shakespeare and the Energies of Drama (Princeton: Princeton Univ. Press, 1972),p.137;see also D.G. James, The Dream of Prospero, pp. 141-47.

175

The relaxation of pace between I.i. and I.ii. ushers in a sustained period of stasis and suspension. The play moves as we bridge the recurring gaps in conversation and pauses in activity that are induced by the magic. For all its presentation of the unities, and of one swift act of the poet's or magician's mind, there is a sense of leisure about The Tempest, as though some strong hand were holding back time's swift foot. This is the antithesis of the hasty Macbeth. The Tempest's moment of transformation is like the interior, slow movement of a larger work: the play's irregular rhythms, lulls and intermittent bursts of energy, its thunder and lightning between periods of quiet, are all miniature renditions of the single interruption that generates the play.[36]

Thus Peterson's apprehension of the play as a moment of critical choice for Prospero oversimplifies the facts.[37] Crisis is everywhere, like surprise in A Midsummer Night's Dream, immanent rather than imminent: this tends to dissipate its force. Prospero's repeated punctuation of action, as at the beginning of Act V, confirms this double truth. Prospero and Ariel enter before Prospero's cell and

---

[36] Clifford Leech,"The Structure of the Last Plays," Shakespeare Survey, 11 (1958),25-27, views the play as a single crisis point in the flux of time on either side of the play, but notes also the muted quality of its conflicts.

[37] Douglas Peterson, Time, Tide and Tempest: A Study of Shakespeare's Romances (San Marino: Huntingdon, 1973), pp. 220-28, thinks Prospero's "decision to forgive is ... not a foregone conclusion."

176

Prospero opens the conversation:

> Now does my project gather to a head:
> My charms crack not; my spirits obey, and time
> Goes upright with his carriage.(V.i.1-3)

True to form, Prospero asks Ariel what time it is, and Ariel replies that it is the sixth hour, "at which time, my lord,/You said our work should cease." More is involved here than recapitulation. Prospero tells us what the play's action has not made us feel (because there is so little action), that this finally is the climactic moment. But if we remember the last lines of Act IV then the first lines of Act V are redundant:

> At this hour
> Lies at my mercy all mine enemies:
> Shortly shall all my labours end... (IV.i.262-64)

The two conversations occur in the same place, and all that lies between them is an act division. Was there perhaps a musical interlude between? Is this a textual aberration due to revision? Or is Shakespeare making a point about Prospero's insistence on the time?[38] Whatever the answer, the repetition diminishes the urgency Prospero would convey. The play's intense dramatic present is neither wholly critical nor static, but a curious compound of tempest within and temperateness without. The characters' single most revolutionary afternoon is also a healing interlude.

---

[38] Kermode's annotation to IV.i.266 reproduces Greg's argument that nothing is missing between the acts.

In other words, Prospero's (and Shakespeare's) magic interrupts the "real" action that the characters are accustomed to playing, and reconstitutes such action as, and in, an artist's idealizing vision. Since visions, particularly improving ones, must be seen if they are to be effective, and since even magic visions fade without an audience, it follows that the magician fails if he cannot elicit some response to his vision: his reconciliation of real and ideal cannot be sustained after he is gone without our help. The magician's success depends on his abandoning exclusive control of his medium, seizing instead what Auden called, in a different spirit perhaps, "The power to enchant/That comes from disillusion."[39] Just as the collapse of the masque empowers Ferdinand and Miranda to body forth the Idea of themselves that they have just contemplated in the vision, so the courtiers can learn to be what Prospero's art would make them, if they will.

And we too are enfranchised when the magician's abdication makes us carry on turning to shapes the airy nothings he has shown us. Our imaginations, "as thin of substance as the air,"[40] are now put to service, much as

[39] W.H. Auden, "The Sea and the Mirror," I, in his The Collected Poetry of W.H. Auden (New York: Random House, 1945), pp. 353-54; Karol Berger, "Prospero's Art," pp.236-37, agrees that "Magic must be abjured before it can become truly operative," that is, must be imposed on the belief of the spectator;

[40] Romeo and Juliet, I.iv.99 (Arden); I owe the connection to Hallett Smith, Shakespeare's Romances: A Study of Some Ways of the Imagination (San Marino: Huntingdon, 1972), p. 130.

178

Prospero's spirit Ariel has been, to the task of realizing Prospero's magic. Pragmatic explanations centering on the controversial nature of magic as it was perceived in Shakespeare's England do not, by the time we reach The Tempest, come anywhere near answering the complex feelings aroused by the abjuration speech. As he unwittingly did in his revels' end speech, Prospero at V.i. reconstitutes the magic that is supposed to be dissolving. He even repeats the image of dissolution, connecting the final suspension of his magic power with the suspensions he has engineered during the play. Addressing the elves

> that on the sand with printless foot
> Do chase the ebbing Neptune, and do fly him
> When he comes back, (V.i.33-35)

Prospero identifies his magic with the control of Neptune, the sea, and tempests: his art can blur the distinction between sea and sky, set roaring war between the green sea and the azured vault. His magic can, in short, dissolve the world in cleansing water.

It is into a watery grave, also fathoms deep, that Prospero casts the book that is symbol of his magic:

> this rough magic
> I here abjure; and, when I have requir'd
> Some heavenly music, -- which even now I do, --
> To work mine end upon their senses, that
> This airy charm is for, I'll break my staff,
> Bury it certain fadoms in the earth
> And deeper than did ever plummet sound,
> I'll drown my book. (V.i.50-57)

The persistence of the imagery of dissolving through the scene and the play indicates its centrality in the Tempest magic. "The charm dissolves apace" (64) after Prospero's abjuration speech, "as the morning steals upon the night,/Melting the darkness" (65-66). The cease of magic and the unclouding of his victims' understanding are simultaneously imaged as the triumph of water over land.

> their understanding
> Begins to swell; and the approaching tide
> Will shortly fill the reasonable shore
> That now lies foul and muddy. (79-82)

Magic dissolves into the sea, as it were, to rush upon the minds of the courtiers like Pericles' great sea of joy, prompting the discoveries that overwhelm and emancipate the self. Prospero's magic, having dissolved the boundaries between real and unreal in the visions, now dissolves itself, removing the last barrier between our imaginations and what imagination can do. Magic has been contained in the better nature of its own making; the magician has given us his own ability to cross what boundaries we please.

The power released by Prospero's relinquishment of magic does not depend on rhetorical device. The courtiers are even more amazed by Prospero's explanations than they were under his spell. The magician's rhetorical efforts to distance them from the power of enchantment by admitting the source actually enhance it. Prospero has arranged that the courtiers shall wake in full possession of "their clearer reason" (68). Gonzalo wakes first, but what he says shows his appreciation of the irrational elements of his sojourn on the island:

> All torment, trouble, wonder and amazement
> Inhabits here: some heavenly power guide us
> Out of this fearful country! (104-6)

Alonso suspects some influence of magic, wondering, as he sees Prospero, "Whether thou be'st he or no,/Or some enchanted trifle to abuse me" (111-12). The courtiers have a far stronger sense than the waking lovers of A Midsummer Night's Dream that some supernatural agency has interfered in their history. Alonso continues: "this must crave -- An if this be at all -- A most strange story" (116-7).

The strangeness of Prospero's story lies in its richness of metaphor, which Alonso does not initially perceive. Prospero's sentences are loaded with double entendres that the courtiers do not catch. He tells Alonso that he too has lost a child "in this last tempest" (153). This is metaphorically true, and as true as Alonso's loss of Ferdinand: both children are lost to the older generation not by premature death but by their greater expectations of the future. Alonso's understanding is still limited to the letter of reality; Prospero also speaks the figurative language of art. The courtiers learn that more complex language, paradoxically, only when they learn of the lovers' survival: they discover metaphor when faced with realities.

181

For the discovery of Ferdinand and Miranda playing at chess in Prospero's cave is the revelation of another spectacle, in the "discovery space" or inner stage. Their "reality" (such as it ever is) has visibly been consumed, as it were, in their status as works of wonder and art.[41] The show of the lovers, like the masque that engendered it, directly addresses its spectators in accents of admiration. Miranda exclaims in wonder at the marvels of creation she sees before her: "O wonder!/How many goodly creatures are there here!" The inhabitants of this "brave new world" are not, as Prospero drily notes, as wonderful as all that; yet their deficiencies make little impact on the scene, and we are moved to wonder if the courtiers will ever become thus artistically ideal and address us, as Miranda does them.

All Prospero's deflationary energies fall short of their target. He indicates that his narrative will, shortly, deliver all: yet his narrative power is subject to strange disturbance. As far back as I.ii. he found himself constantly interrupting his exposition to Miranda to ask her if she was listening: his anxiety is odd, since few fathers can have had daughters as attentive. "Dost thou attend me?" (78) he asks, and the query recurs at lines 87 ("Thou attend'st not") and 106 ("Dost thou hear?"). Even before Prospero's magic breaks Miranda's engagement with him in conversation by putting her to sleep, something, perhaps

[41] Julian Patrick, "The Tempest as Supplement," p. 176, makes this beautifully clear.

also magic, interferes with the momentum of the history her father relates. Prospero's claim to be able to "discourse wonders" (Bottom's phrase) at the end of the play is jeopardized by a similar pattern of interruption, and the claim is never fully realized. The result of his effort is at odds with his narrative purpose, increasing not decreasing the strangeness, introducing more punctuation than conjunction into the story, and his exposition is, again, curiously piecemeal:

> howsoe'er you have
> Been justled from your senses, know for certain
> That I am Prospero, and that very duke
> Which was thrust forth of Milan, who most strangely
> Upon this shore, where you were wrack'd was landed,
> To be the lord on't. No more yet of this;
> For 'tis a chronicle of day by day,
> Not a relation for a breakfast, nor
> Befitting this first meeting.(157-66)

Again, Prospero declares he will explain the "happen'd accidents" (250) in a way that will clarify everything:

> Do not infest your mind with beating in
> The strangeness of this business; at pick'd leisure
> Which shall be shortly single, I'll resolve you
> Which to you shall seem probable, of every
> These happen'd accidents; till when, be cheerful,
> And think of each thing well. (246-51)

At the end, once again, he announces his plan to tell

> the story of my life
> And the particular accidents gone by
> Since I came to this isle.(304-306)

The story is not told during the play, at least to the courtiers.

183

The play's "particular accidents" are not as easily told as its general shape. Prospero's magic manipulation of the events of the four hours on the island cannot be explained in the probable, rational terms of narrative form. Every narrative impulse of Prospero's recreates the mysteries he tries to dispel. The explanations are introduced primarily, I believe, to prove their inadequacy. "These are not natural events," says Alonso, newly wise: "they strengthen/From strange to stranger" (227). They are communicable not through scientific equations or logical syllogism but in the analogies of creative art.

And so the play's ending dispels only the possibility of disenchantment. Its magic, independent of the magician, and not reducible to something we can fully comprehend, is not dissolved when the magician "explains" it. Prospero's fragmentary explanations in the last act may be interpreted as a desire to prolong the action he controls: Harry Berger sees the last scene as an endless ending.[42] This ending, like that of A Midsummer Night's Dream, also recalls the beginnings of the action, in spite of Prospero's injunction: "Let us not burthen our remembrance with/A heaviness that's gone" (199-200). Comedy requires that the cast reassemble on stage, and that the end

[42] Harry Berger, "Miraculous Harp: A Reading of Shakespeare's The Tempest," Shakespeare Studies, 5 (1970 for 69), 277-78.

of the action forget not its beginning, but The Tempest reinforces these standard structural circularities. When Ariel enters with the ship's crew, Gonzalo recalls his gallows humor of the tempest scene. The tempest of scene one repeats for the courtiers something like Prospero's experience of twelve years before. Prospero's plans for his return resemble the retirement that originally caused his exile. Yet we know that when he says that every third thought will be his grave, he does not mean the same thing as his original neglect of worldly ends.

The play's consistent recollection of earlier action does more than draw the circle of its action just: the play is a magic circle, and duration takes on magical dimensions. History is itself transformed: its dramatic reenactment is an artistic rewriting of the past that at once mirrors and remakes it. Shakespeare, finally, breaks through the boundaries Sidney drew for poetry: the poet "never maketh any circles about your imagination, to conjure you to believe for true, what he writeth" (p. 136). The Tempest does conjure us to believe that its fictions may come true, and that history and legend, nature and art, may fuse.

For Prospero's art can subsist beyond the island's magic circle, the wooden O, and can if we help translate the great globe itself. The play is framed by a releasing as well as a confining action: the circle can, as it were, infinitely expand, inscribing us with the courtiers (V.i.33ff),

185

transfiguring us all.  Prospero frees Ariel from confinement
twice, twelve years before the play opens, and again when it
ends:

it was mine Art,
When I arriv'd and heard thee, that made gape
The pine, and let thee out (I.ii.290-93)

says Prospero.  And at the end he "discases" himself by
magic from the spiritual bondage that has divorced him from
his fellow men.

We are, in the last analysis, enclosed within the circle,
invited to become the magician.  Prospero, having pardoned
and freed his subordinate, Ariel, immediately subordinates
himself to us, in the epilogue.  He asks us to release him:
"Let your indulgence set me free."  Now that his charms are
all overthrown, his power devolves to us, and we may confine
him on the island, as he did Ariel, by a simple "spell."
Prospero's last words draw us into the play, make us its
chief character and author.  The limits of the _Tempest_ magic
are ours -- and so are its possibilities.  Authority, even a
magician's, may be most powerful when humbly without
"Spirits to enforce, Art to enchant."  It is this power we
are offered:  the sympathetic magic of a generous
imagination, transforming  natural constraints into a
strange freedom.

Ariel's full fadom five song tells how even the greatest
of our constraints, death itself, may dissolve in
intimations of immortality.  Ariel records the

186

transformation of drowned men into artifacts, and crystallizes the significant achievement of the play:

> Nothing of him that doth fade
> But doth suffer a sea-change
> Into something rich and strange. (I.ii.402-404)

Alonso drowns only figuratively. His spiritual reconstitution, however, is quite literally achieved only insofar as he approaches the condition of art, as he becomes one of the wonders that Miranda admires (and Prospero indicates that her optimism may be premature). Magic is, as Brower saw, essentially sea-change,[43] and in The Tempest it is the instant of dissolving into purifying water that creates the artifact. The self-consuming of this play's art in the apparent dissolution of its magic constitutes a promise not a threat. Here, that "There is no truth beyond magic"[44] is a subject for rejoicing. Michael Goldman writes that "Enchantment and disenchantment are a twin birth of our awareness of limitation. We discover the most truth about ourselves by attempting to grasp the phantoms we create, which fade into thin air."[45] Shakespeare educates, literally, by leading us out of ourselves into the magic world of his art, out of certainties into mystery: The

[43] R. Brower, "The Mirror of Analogy," pp. 420-29, and notes also the central image of dissolving.

[44] John Fowles, The Magus, Revised Version (Boston: Little, Brown & Co., 1977), p. 552.

[45] Goldman, Shakespeare and the Energies of Drama, p. 150.

187

<u>Tempest</u> allows us temporarily to wonder if its discovery of our limitations may not also be, in sober truth, the means of our release from them. There can scarcely be a greater magic than this.

And not even the greatest of English stage magicians could, after this, do more. Shakespeare, as we have seen, stands as the culmination of dramatic magic. From Friar Bacon to Prospero, the magus himself undergoes a dramatic transformation. He focusses on stage a whole history of popular belief, societal suspicion, and intellectual aspiration and caveats. The magician in Marlowe, Greene and Peele, is confined by all the conflicting estimates of his craft that were current in the sixteenth century. The dramatist's construction of the magician in these early plays mirrors the prejudices, beliefs and nascent skepticism of his age, and the artist's identification with the magician is inhibited by contemporary controversies about the power and fitness of magic to ameliorate nature. The temporal discontinuities wrought by the magician on dramatic action may reflect Renaissance anxieties about time as much as they suggest unrealities and work miracles: the magician, like the divine arbiter of our progress through life, can destroy as well as confirm our hopes, and, like Sidney's <u>vates</u>, requires constant and vigorous defense. But the early dramatic magicians in the period, Sacrapant and

Bacon, are inadequately defended by their authors, and are defeated in order that some ideal may be realized in the ending. Even Faustus, more explicitly and completely like his dramatist-creator, suffers a loss in the end, though Marlowe portrays this as tragedy.

Shakespeare arrives on the scene before magic leaves the popular imagination, yet, always in advance of his time, transforms the magician more completely than any playwright before or since into the quintessence of the artist. Beginning hesitantly and partially in A Midsummer Night's Dream to identify himself with the magic and supernatural forces he dramatizes, he arrives in The Tempest at a more provocative defense of art and a more profound synthesis of dramatic structure with magic principles than was possible in the lighter vein of the earlier comedy.

Shakespeare's magic is even more intrinsic to the fabric of his vision than is the magic of his predecessors on the stage: Shakespeare's magician controls time and space with, increasingly, the finesse of his master. Shakespeare's portrait of the sympathetic magician zeroes in ever more closely on the precise means and ends of the magus' enterprise, and the magician becomes more sympathetic, whiter, than Faustus, Bacon, or Sacrapant. The ostensible rejection by the magician of his power thus poses a different problem from that in Greene's and Peele's plays, where the morality of the magician's operations is always

189

tacitly assumed to be ambiguous at best. Shakespeare's formidable conquest of this difficulty confirms the power of art to transcend limits and become truly magical, fusing golden with brazen nature. The gentle qualification of fairy power in A Midsummer Night's Dream is in The Tempest translated in Prospero's fully-fledged renunciation of magic; the true poignance of his abjuration, though, lies not in the debilitation of one magician but in the hard fact that the perpetuation of magic is not inevitable. It is ours to command or to forget.

Shakespeare thus transfigures magician into serious artist, magic into imagination. As belief systems in the real England of the seventeenth century begin to falter on the rocks of a new empiricism and disenchanted science, Shakespeare inscribes the magic that is fading from the world into the second world of his art.[46] If magicians in the Jacobean period lose ground to their more scientific counterparts, yet imagination is the richer. the potential in art to transform and enlarge a shrinking world is in Shakespeare's Tempest attributable directly and wholly to magicians; they compel belief not just in themselves, nor in their art, but in ourselves.

So we have slowly gained, through the maturing of magical comedy in the English Renaissance, a genuine advantage over Spenser's Calidore and Colin Clout, who usher in the period,

[46] D.G. James, The Dream of Prospero, pp. 66-67, makes a similar suggestion.

190

and were so credited at the beginning of my study. They can only mourn when the Graces of The Faerie Queene, VI.x., vanish, immediately, under scrutiny. By the time Shakespeare completes his Tempest, our power to see and sustain "enchaunted shows" is immeasurably superior; the author commands our eyes, and our presence, unlike Calidore's, is not inimical to his magic. We do not dissipate but perpetuate the show by engaging in it. We stand now within the magic circle,[47] the position denied by Spenser both to Calidore and Colin. Shakespeare places us in the magical world of imagination, whose margins fade forever and forever as we move.

---

[47] Barbara L. Estrin, "Telling the Magician from the Magic in The Tempest," in Bucknell Review: Shakespeare: Contemporary Critical Approaches, ed. H.R. Garvin (Lewisburg: Bucknell Univ. Press, 1980), p. 173, notes the Calidore episode in conjunction with the magic circle in The Tempest.

# Works Cited

Adams, Hazard. _Critical Theory Since Plato_. New York: Harcourt, 1971.

Aristotle. _Poetics_. Tr. Ingram Bywater. With preface by Gilbert Murray. Oxford: Clarendon Press, 1954.

Agrippa, Henry Cornelius. _The Philosophy of Natural Magic_. 1531; rpt. Secaucus: University Books, 1974.

Arnold, Paul. _Clef pour Shakespeare: Esoterisme de L'oeuvre Shakespearienne_. Paris: Librairie Philosophique J. Vrin, 1977.

Arnold, Paul. _Esoterisme de Shakespeare_. Paris: Mercure de France, 1955.

Arthos, John. _Shakespeare's Use of Dream and Vision_. London: Bowes, 1977.

Auden, W. H. _The Collected Poetry of W. H. Auden_. New York: Random House, 1945.

Bacon, Francis. _The Advancement of Learning_. In _The Advancement of Learning and New Atlantis_. Ed. Thomas Case. London: Oxford Univ. Press, 1906, 1974.

Barber, C. L. _Shakespeare's Festive Comedy: A Study of Dramatic Form and Its Relation to Social Custom_. Princeton: Princeton Univ. Press, 1959.

Barton, Anne, ed. _The Tempest_. Harmondsworth: Penguin, 1981.

Beckerman, Bernard. _Dynamics of Drama: Theory and Method of Analysis_. 1970; rpt. New York: Drama Book Specialist, 1979.

Berger, Harry, Jr. "Miraculous Harp: A Reading of Shakespeare's The Tempest." _Shakespeare Studies_, 5 (1970 for 69), 253-93.

Berger, Harry, Jr. "The Renaissance Imagination: Second World and Green World." _Centennial Review_, 9 (Winter 1965), 36-78.

192

Berger, Karol. "Prospero's Art." Shakespeare Studies, 10 (1977), 211-39.

Bergson, Henri. "Laughter." In Comedy. Ed. Wylie Sypher. Baltimore: Johns Hopkins Univ. Press, 1956, pp. 61-190.

Blake, William. "The Marriage of Heaven and Hell." In Selected Poetry and Prose of Blake. Ed. Northrop Frye. New York: Modern Library, 1953.

Booth, Stephen, ed. Shakespeare's Sonnets. New Haven: Yale Univ. Press, 1977.

Bradbrook, Muriel C. "Peele's Old Wives' Tale: A Play of Enchantment." English Studies, 43 (1962), 323-30.

Briggs, K. M. Pale Hecate's Team: An Examination of the Beliefs on Witchcraft and Magic Among Shakespeare's Contemporaries and His Immediate Successors. London: Routledge and Kegan Paul, 1962.

Brower, Reuben A. "The Mirror of Analogy: The Tempest." Rpt. in Shakespeare's Later Comedies: An Anthology of Modern Criticism. Ed. D. J. Palmer. Harmondsworth: Penguin, 1971, pp. 404-31.

Champion, Larry S. The Evolution of Shakespeare's Comedy. Cambridge: Harvard Univ. Press, 1970.

Cheffaud, P. H. George Peele. Paris: Librarie Felix Alcan, 1913.

Cinthio, Giraldi. Discorso intorno al comporre dei romanzi. Tr. H. L. Snuggs. Lexington: Univ. of Kentucky Press, 1968.

Coghill, Nevill. "The Basis of Shakespearian Comedy." In Shakespeare Criticism 1935-60. Ed. Anne Ridler. London: Oxford Univ. Press, 1963, pp. 201-27.

Coleridge, Samuel Taylor. Essays and Lectures on Shakespeare and Some Other Poets and Dramatists. London: Dent, n.d.

Cook, Albert. Shakespeare's Enactment: The Dynamics of Renaissance Theatre. Chicago: Swallow Press, 1970.

193

Cope, Jackson. *The Theater and the Dream: From Metaphor to Form in Renaissance Drama*. Baltimore: Johns Hopkins Univ. Press, 1973.

Danson, Lawrence. "Christopher Marlowe: The Questioner." *ELR* (Winter 1982), 3-29.

Dent, R. W. "Imagination in *A Midsummer Night's Dream*." *Shakespeare Quarterly*, 15.2 (1964), 115-29.

Doran, Madeleine. *Endeavors of Art: A Study of Form in Elizabethan Drama*. Madison: Univ. of Wisconsin Press, 1954.

Edwards, Philip. *Shakespeare and the Confines of Art*. London: Methuen, 1968.

Egan, Robert. *Drama Within Drama*. New York: Columbia Univ. Press, 1975.

Eggers, Walter F., Jr. "'Bring forth a wonder': Presentation in Shakespeare's Romances." *TSLL*, 21 (1979), 455-77.

Estrin, Barbara L. "Telling the Magician from the Magic in *The Tempest*." In *Bucknell Review: Shakespeare: Contemporary Critical Approaches*. Ed. H. R. Garvin. Lewisburg: Bucknell Univ. Press, 1980, pp. 170-87.

Ettin, Andrew V. "Magic into Art: The Magician's Renunciation of Magic in English Renaissance Drama." *TSLL*, 19 (1977), 268-93.

Felperin, Howard. *Shakespearean Romance*. Princeton: Princeton Univ. Press, 1972.

Fergusson, Francis. *The Idea of a Theater*. Princeton: Princeton Univ. Press, 1949.

Fineman, Daniel A. *Maurice Morgann: Shakespearian Criticism*. Oxford: Clarendon Press, 1972.

Force, Peter, ed. *Tracts and Other Papers*. Vol. 3. Washington: Peter Force, 1836-46.

Fowles, John. *The Magus, Revised Version*. Boston: Little, Brown and Co., 1977.

Frazer, J. G. *The Golden Bough: A Study in Magic and Religion*. One-vol. abridged ed. New York: Macmillan, 1951.

194

Frye, Northrop. *The Anatomy of Criticism*. Princeton: Princeton Univ. Press, 1957.

Frye, Northrop. "The Argument of Comedy." Rpt. in *Shakespeare: Modern Essays in Criticism*. Ed. L. F. Dean. New York: Oxford, 1957, pp. 79-89.

Frye, Northrop. "Romance as Masque." In his *Spiritus Mundi: Essays on Literature, Myth, and Society*. Bloomington: Indiana Univ. Press, 1976, pp. 148-73.

Frye, Northrop. *The Secular Scripture: A Study of the Structure of Romance*. Cambridge: Harvard Univ. Press, 1976.

Garber, Marjorie B. *Dream in Shakespeare: From Metaphor to Metamorphosis*. New Haven: Yale Univ. Press, 1974.

Gardner, Helen. "As You Like It." In *More Talking of Shakespeare*. Ed. J. Garrett. Freeport: Books for Libraries Press, 1970, pp. 17-32.

Giamatti, A. Bartlett. "Spenser: From Magic to Miracle." In *Four Essays in Romance*. Ed. Herschel Baker. Cambridge: Harvard Univ. Press, 1971, pp. 15-31.

Godshalk, W. L. *The Marlovian World Picture*. The Hague: Mouton, 1974.

Goldman, Michael. *Shakespeare and the Energies of Drama*. Princeton: Princeton Univ. Press, 1972.

Greene, Gayle. "'Excellent Dumb Discourse': Silence and Grace in Shakespeare's *Tempest*." *Studia Neophilologica*, 50 (1978), 193-205.

Greene, Robert. *Friar Bacon and Friar Bungay*. Ed. Daniel Seltzer. Lincoln: Univ. of Nebraska Press, 1963.

Greene, Robert. *Orlando Furioso*. In *The Plays and Poems of Robert Greene*. Vol. 1. Ed. J. Churton Collins. Oxford: Clarendon Press, 1905.

Greg, W. W. "The Damnation of Faustus." Rpt. in *Marlowe: A Collection of Critical Essays*. Ed. Clifford Leech. Englewood Cliffs, NJ: Prentice-Hall, 1964, pp. 92-107.

Greg, W. W., ed. *Marlowe's Doctor Faustus, 1604-1616: Parallel Text*. Oxford: Clarendon Press, 1950.

Hasler, Jorg. *Shakespeare's Theatrical Notation: The Comedies*. Bern: Franck, 1974.

195

Hatnaway, Baxter. _Marvels and Commonplaces: Renaissance Literary Criticism_. New York: Random House, 1968.

Hawkins, Sherman H. "The Two Worlds of Shakespearean Comedy." _Shakespeare Studies_, 3 (1967), 62-80.

Henze, Richard. "_A Midsummer Night's Dream_: Analogous Image." _Shakespeare Studies_, 7 (1974), 115-23.

Hibbard, George R. "Adumbrations of _The Tempest_ in _A Midsummer Night's Dream_." _Shakespeare Survey_, 31 (1978), 77-83.

Hirsch, James E. _The Structure of Shakespearean Scenes_. New Haven: Yale Univ. Press, 1981.

Holland, Norman. "Hermia's Dream." In _Representing Shakespeare: New Psychoanalytic Essays_. Ed. Murray Schwartz and Coppelia Kahn. Baltimore: Jonns Hopkins Univ. Press, 1980, pp. 1-20.

Homan, Sidney. _When the Theater Turns to Itself: The Aesthetic Metaphor in Shakespeare_. Lewisourg: Bucknell Univ. Press, 1981.

Huston, J. Dennis. _Shakespeare's Comedies of Play_. New York: Columbia Univ. Press, 1981.

James, D. G. _The Dream of Prospero_. Oxford: Clarendon Press, 1967.

Jameson, Frederic. _The Political Unconscious: Narrative as a Socially Symbolic Act_. Ithaca: Cornell Univ. Press, 1981.

Jenkins, Harold. "Peele's 'Old Wive's Tale.'" _ILR_, 34 (1939), 177-85.

Jewkes, W. T. "'Excellent Dumb Discourse': The Limits of Language in _The Tempest_." In _Essays on Snakespeare_. Ed. Gordon Ross Smith. Univ. Park: Pennsylvania State Univ. Press, 1965, pp. 196-210.

Jonson, Ben. _The Alchemist_. In _Ben Jonson_. Vol. 5. Eds. C. H. Herford, Percy Simpson, and Evelyn Simpson. Oxford Clarendon Press, 1937.

Jonson, Ben. _Every Man in His Humour_ [1616]. In _Ben Jonson_. Vol. 3. Eds. C. H. Herford, Percy Simpson, and Evelyn Simpson. Oxford: Clarendon Press, 1927.

Kermode, Frank. *The Final Plays*. London: Longmans for British Council, 1963. Rpt. in his *Shakespeare, Spenser, Donne*. London: Routledge, 1971.

Kermode, Frank, ed. *Othello*. In *The Riverside Shakespeare*. Ed. G. Blakemore Evans. Boston: Houghton Mifflin, 1974.

Kermode, Frank. *The Sense of an Ending: Studies in the Theory of Fiction*. New York: Oxford Univ. Press, 1967.

Kernan, Alvin, ed. *Othello*. In *The Complete Signet Classic Shakespeare*. Ed. Sylvan Barnet. New York: Harcourt, 1972.

Kernan, Alvin. *The Playwright as Magician: Shakespeare's Image of the Poet in the English Public Theater*. New Haven: Yale Univ. Press, 1979.

Knights, L. C. "The Orthodoxy of *Faustus*." In *Twentieth-Century Interpretations of Doctor Faustus*. Ed. Willard Farnham. Englewood Cliffs, NJ: Prentice-Hall, 1969, pp. 97-100.

Knights, L. C. "The Tempest." In *Shakespeare's Late Plays: Essays in Honor of Charles Crow*. Ed. C. Tobias and P. G. Zolbrod. Athens: Ohio Univ. Press, 1974, pp. 15-31.

Kris, Ernest and Otto Kurz. *Legend, Myth, and Magic in the Image of the Artist*. With Preface by E. H. Gombrich. New Haven: Yale Univ. Press, 1979.

Langer, Susanne. *Feeling and Form: A Theory of Art*. New York: Scribner's, 1953.

Leech, Clifford. "The Structure of the Last Plays." *Shakespeare Survey*, 11 (1958), 18-30.

Leggatt, Alexander. *Shakespeare's Comedy of Love*. London: Methuen, 1974.

Levin, Harry. *The Overreacher: A Study of Christopher Marlowe*. Cambridge: Harvard Univ. Press, 1952.

Levin, Richard. *The Multiple Plot in English Renaissance Drama*. Chicago: Univ. of Chicago Press, 1971.

Lewis, C. S. *English Literature in the Sixteenth Century*. London: Oxford Univ. Press, 1954.

Marlowe, Christopher. _Doctor Faustus_. Ed. Roma Gill. London: Bener, 1965.

Marx, Joan C. "'Soft, Who Have We Here?': The Dramatic Technique of _The Old Wives Tale_." _Renaissance Drama_, n.s. 12 (1981), 117-43.

Masinton, Charles G. _Christopher Marlowe's Tragic Vision_. Athens: Ohio Univ. Press, 1972.

McNulty, Robert, ed. _Orlando Furioso_. By Ariosto. Tr. into English heroical verse by Sir John Harington [1591]. Oxford: Clarendon Press, 1972.

Mowat, Barbara. _The Dramaturgy of Shakespeare's Romances_. Athens: Univ. of Georgia Press, 1976.

Nicoll, Allardyce. "Shakespeare and the Court Masque." _Shakespeare Jahrbuch_, 94 (1958), 51-62.

Nuttall, A. D. _Two Concepts of Allegory: A Study of Shakespeare's The Tempest and the Logic of Allegorical Expression_. London: Routledge and Kegan Paul, 1967.

Orgel, Stephen. _The Illusion of Power: Political Theater in the English Renaissance_. Berkeley: Univ. of California Press, 1975.

Orgel, Stephen. "New Uses of Adversity: Tragic Experience in _The Tempest_." In _In Defense of Reading: A Reader's Approach to Literary Criticism_. Ed. R. Brower and R. Poirier. New York: Dutton, 1962, pp. 110-32.

Palmer, D. J. "Magic and Poetry in _Doctor Faustus_." Revised and rpt. in _Marlowe: Doctor Faustus: A Casebook_. Ed. John Jump. London: Macmillan, 1969, pp. 188-203.

Paolucci, Anne. "The Lost Days in _A Midsummer Night's Dream_." _Shakespeare Quarterly_, 28.3 (1977), 317-26.

Patrick, Julian. "'The Tempest' as Supplement." In _Centre and Labyrinth: Essays in Honour of Northrop Frye_. Ed. E. Cook, C. Hosek, J. Macpherson, P. Parker, J. Patrick. Toronto: Univ. of Toronto Press, 1982, pp. 162-80.

Peele, George. _The Araygnment of Paris_. Ed. R. Mark Benbow. In _The Dramatic Works of George Peele_. Vol. 3 of _The Life and Works of George Peele_. Ed. Charles T. Prouty. New Haven: Yale Univ. Press, 1970.

198

Peele, George. *The Old Wives Tale*. Ed. Frank S. Hook.
In *The Dramatic Works of George Peele*. Vol. 3 of
*The Life and Works of George Peele*. Ed. Charles T.
Prouty. New Haven: Yale Univ. Press, 1970.

Peterson, Douglas. *Time, Tide, and Tempest: A Study of
Shakespeare's Romances*. San Marino: Huntingdon, 1973.

Peterson, Richard S. *Imitation and Praise in the Poems
of Ben Jonson*. New Haven: Yale Univ. Press, 1981.

Poulet, Georges. *Studies in Human Time*. Tr. Elliott
Coleman. 1956; rpt. New York, 1959.

Reed, Robert Rentoul, Jr. *The Occult on the Tudor and
Stuart Stage*. Boston: Christopher Publishing House,
1965.

Righter, Anne. *Shakespeare and the Idea of Play*.
New York: Barnes and Noble, 1962.

Scholes, R. and R. Kellogg. *The Nature of Narrative*.
New York: Oxford Univ. Press, 1966.

Scott, W. O. *The God of Arts: Ruling Ideas in
Shakespeare's Comedies*. Lawrence: University
of Kansas Publications, 1977.

Scragg, Leah. "Shakespeare, Lyly and Ovid: The Influence
of 'Gallathea' on 'A Midsummer Night's Dream.'"
*Shakespeare Survey*, 30 (1977), 125-34.

Shakespeare, William. *King Henry VIII*. Ed. R. A. Foakes.
London: Methuen, 1957.

Shakespeare, William. *King Lear*. Ed. Kenneth Muir.
London: Methuen, 1959.

Shakespeare, William. *A Midsummer Night's Dream*.
Ed. Harold F. Brooks. London: Methuen, 1979.

Shakespeare, William. *Pericles*. Ed. F. D. Hoeniger.
London: Methuen, 1963.

Shakespeare, William. *Romeo and Juliet*. Ed. Brian
Gibbons. London: Methuen, 1980.

Shakespeare, William. *The Tempest*. Ed. Frank Kermode.
London: Methuen, 1954, 58.

Shakespeare, William. *The Winter's Tale*. Ed. J. H. P.
Pafford. London: Methuen, 1963.

Sherbo, Artnur, ed. *Johnson on Shakespeare*. Vol. 8 of
*The Yale Edition of the Works of Samuel Johnson*.
Gen. ed. W. Jackson Bate. New Haven: Yale Univ.
Press, 1968.

Sidney, Pnilip. *The Defence of Poesy*. In *Sir Philip
Sidney: Selected Prose and Poetry*. Ed. Robert
Kimbrough. San Francisco: Rinehart, 1969.

Smith, Hallett. *Shakespeare's Romances: A Study of Some
Ways of the Imagination*. San Marino: Huntingdon,
1972.

Smith, Irwin. "Ariel and the Masque in *The Tempest*."
*Shakespeare Quarterly*, 21 (1970), 213-22.

Spenser, Edmund. *The Faerie Queene*. Ed. Thomas P. Roche,
Jr. New Haven: Yale Univ. Press, 1978.

Steane, J. B. *Marlowe: A Critical Study*. Cambridge:
The Univ. Press, 1964.

Stevens, Wallace. *The Necessary Angel*. 1951; rpt.
London: Faber, 1960.

Taylor, Michael. "The Darker Purpose of *A Midsummer
Night's Dream*." *SEL*, 9 (1969), 259-73.

Tennyson, Alfred Lord. "Ulysses." In *The Poems and Plays
of Alfred Lord Tennyson*. New York: Modern Library,
1938.

Thomas, Keith. *Religion and the Decline of Magic*.
Harmondsworth: Penguin, 1971, 1973.

Tillyard, E. M. W. *Shakespeare's Late Plays*. 1938; rpt.
New York: Barnes and Noble, 1964.

Warren, Michael J. "*Doctor Faustus*: The Old Man and the
Text." *ELR*, 11.2 (1981), 111-47.

Weinberg, Bernard. *A History of Literary Criticism in
the Italian Renaissance*. Vol. 2. Chicago: Univ.
of Chicago Press, 1961.

West, Robert Hunter. *The Invisible World: A Study of
Pneumatology in Elizabethan Drama*. Athens, GA:
Univ. of Georgia Press, 1939.

West, Robert Hunter. *Shakespeare and the Outer Mystery*.
Lexington: Univ. of Kentucky Press, 1968.

Wilkinson, Henry C. *The Adventurers of Bermuda*. 2nd ed. London: Oxford Univ. Press, 1958.

Wilson, Dover. *The Meaning of* The Tempest. Newcastle: Literary and Philosophical Society, 1936.

Wilson, J. Dover. *Shakespeare's Happy Comedies*. London: Faber, 1962.

Woodman, David. *White Magic and Elizabethan Renaissance Drama*. Rutherford: Fairleigh Dickinson Univ. Press, 1973.

Wordsworth, William. "Ode: Intimations of Immortality from Recollections of Early Childhood." In *Selected Poems and Prefaces*. Ed. Jack Stillinger. Boston: Houghton Mifflin, 1965.

Wright, L. B., ed. *A Voyage to Virginia in 1609: Two Narratives*. Charlottesville: Univ. Press of Virginia, 1964.

Wright, Neil H. "Reality and Illusion as Philosophical Pattern in *The Tempest*." *Shakespeare Studies*, 10 (1977), 241-70.

Yates, Frances A. *Shakespeare's Last Plays: A New Approach*. London: Routledge, 1975.

Young, David P. *The Hart's Forest: A Study of Shakespeare's Pastoral Plays*. New Haven: Yale Univ. Press, 1972.

Young, David. P. *Something of Great Constancy: The Art of "A Midsummer Night's Dream."* New Haven: Yale Univ. Press, 1966.